THE ULTIMATE FRENCH MONARCHS QUIZ

I0424562

B.R. Egginton

<u>Contents</u>

<u>Prologue</u>

Liberté, égalité, fraternité

Today the French monarchy is best known for its bloody demise: Louis XVI, the French Revolution and the advent of the guillotine.

In the late eighteenth century it was an institution in freefall; brought into disrepute by an incompetent captain at the helm. But this was merely a blip in the long and complicated history of France's kings and queens and produces a distorted vision of their legacy as a whole.

Little under a century before the Sun King had been the embodiment of absolute monarchy: respected, all-powerful, and the sole ruler of Europe's most powerful nation.

If you doubt this, just take one look at the mighty Palace of Versailles and stand corrected. Like the Pyramids of Giza and the Tower of London, it could have been the product of only two things: wealth and power galore.

But their lasting impression on the world went above and beyond architecture. Not only did the French monarchs make France France – uniting her people under one banner – they also spread its language and customs all over the world: from Africa to Asia to the New World. And even in the present day, long after the last coronation took place at Rheims Cathedral, French culture remains a global force.

So what went wrong for France's blue-blooded autocrats?

Find out the answer to that question – and many, many more – inside.

Questions

Clovis I

Q1 Clovis I was King of what?

Q2 What dynasty was Clovis I a part of?

Q3 Who was Clovis I's father?

Q4 What leader did Clovis I face in the Battle of Soissons?

Q5 What religion did Clovis I convert to?

Q6 Who was Clovis I's wife?

Q7 In what year did Clovis I succeed his father as king?

Q8 What city did Clovis I make his capital?

Q9 What key battle did Clovis I fight against the Alamanni?

Q10 How was Audofleda related to Clovis I?

Theuderic I

Q1 Who is believed to have been Theuderic I's wife?

Q2 Who succeeded Theuderic I as king after his death?

Q3 Following Clovis I's death, the kingdom was divided up between Theuderic I and how many of his siblings?

Q4 In what poem does King Hygelac appear?

Q5 Sigismund (died 524) was King of what?

Q6 What abbey did Theuderic I's daughter, Theodechild, establish?

Q7 Where did Theuderic I rule from?

Q8 Which of Theuderic I's brothers inherited Paris after their father's death?

Q9 Theuderic I assisted which King of the Thuringii to defeat his brother?

Q10 In what year did the Battle of Vézeronce take place?

Theudebert I

Q1 Who succeeded Theudebert I as king?

Q2 Who wrote the *History of the Franks*?

Q3 What collection of letters were compiled at the court of the King of Austrasia between the 5th and 7th centuries?

Q4 What king is Theudebert I said to have defeated in circa 516?

Q5 Which Byzantine Emperor started the Gothic War?

Q6 Theudebert I broke imperial custom by minting what?

Q7 How was Wisigard related to Theudebert I?

Q8 Deuteria was an aristocrat from what culture?

Q9 Who did Theudebert I have to fight in order to inherit his father's kingdom?

Q10 What dynasty was Theudebert I a part of?

Theudebald

Q1 Who was Theudebald's wife?

Q2 In what year did Theudebald die?

Q3 How was Theudebert I related to Theudebald?

Q4 Justinian I was Emperor of what during Theudebald's reign?

Q5 Theudebald's wife was the daughter of what king?

Q6 What territory did Theudebald rule over?

Q7 Who succeeded Theudebald as king?

Q8 What did Theudebald suffer from for much of his reign?

Q9 What was the occupation of Narses?

Q10 In what centuries did the Merovingian dynasty rule?

Chlodomer

Q1 Who was Chlodomer's father?

Q2 Chlodomer was King of what?

Q3 Chlodomer was killed in what battle?

Q4 In what year did Chlodomer die?

Q5 How many sons did Chlodomer have with his wife?

Q6 Who were Chlodomer's three brothers?

Q7 Who did Chlodomer's wife later marry?

Q8 Who did Chlodomer have killed in 524?

Q9 Which of Chlodomer's children became a saint?

Q10 What relation succeeded Chlodomer as king?

Childebert I

Q1 Where was Childebert I born?

Q2 Who was Childebert I's mother?

Q3 Following his father's death, Childebert I became King of what?

Q4 In what year did Childebert I become King of Orléans?

Q5 How many of Chlodomer's children were murdered?

Q6 How was Clotilde related to Childebert I?

Q7 How many daughters did Childebert I have with his wife?

Q8 What religion did Childebert I follow?

Q9 Who succeeded Childebert I as king?

Q10 Who was Childebert I's wife?

Chlothar I

Q1 How many wives did Chlothar I have?

Q2 In what year did Chlothar I become King of the Franks?

Q3 Chlothar I became King of what after his father's death?

Q4 What Christian doctrine did Chlothar I flout?

Q5 Which relative of Chlothar I was killed at the Battle of Vézeronce?

Q6 Which sisters were married to Chlothar I?

Q7 How was Theudebert I related to Chlothar I?

Q8 Which of Chlodomer's children did Chlothar I fail to kill?

Q9 In Frankish culture long hair was a symbol of what?

Q10 Which rebellious son did Chlothar I have killed?

Charibert I

Q1 Charibert I served as King of what?

Q2 Who was Charibert I's mother?

Q3 In what year did Charibert I become king?

Q4 How was Ingoberga related to Charibert I?

Q5 What daughter of Charibert I went on to become a saint?

Q6 Charibert I married one of his daughters to what future King of Kent?

Q7 After the death of Charibert I's father, how many brothers did he have to share the inheritance with?

Q8 What happened to Charibert I as a result of him practicing polygamy?

Q9 Where is Charibert I said to have been buried?

Q10 What happened to Charibert I's kingdom after his death?

Guntram

Q1 Guntram was King of what?

Q2 Who was Guntram's father?

Q3 In what years did Guntram rule?

Q4 Guntram was made a what by the Catholic Church?

Q5 Who wrote the *Decem Libri Historiarum*?

Q6 What was the occupation of Mummolus?

Q7 Who did Guntram adopt as his son and heir?

Q8 Gundoald claimed to be an illegitimate son of who?

Q9 Who attempted to assassinate Guntram in 587?

Q10 Where did Guntram die?

Sigebert I

Q1 Who was Sigebert I's wife?

Q2 Sigebert I was King of what?

Q3 Incursions by what nomadic group forced Sigebert I to move his capital from Rheims to Metz?

Q4 Who succeeded Sigebert I as king?

Q5 Ingund was the first Catholic Queen of what?

Q6 How was Chilperic I related to Sigebert I?

Q7 What caused Sigebert I's death?

Q8 Where did Sigebert I die?

Q9 What king had Galswintha murdered?

Q10 In what years did Sigebert I rule?

Childebert II

Q1 Childebert II served as King of what from 592?

Q2 Who was Childebert II's adoptive father?

Q3 In what year did Childebert II die?

Q4 What caused Childebert II's father's death?

Q5 Dynamius was Rector of what?

Q6 In what year was the Treaty of Andelot agreed?

Q7 Childebert II became King of what after his father's death?

Q8 What were Childebert II's two sons called?

Q9 What emperor did Childebert II fight in the name of on a number of occasions?

Q10 Who was Childebert II's mother?

Theudebert II

Q1 How was Brunhilda related to Theudebert II?

Q2 Who was Theudebert II's wife?

Q3 Where was Theudebert II locked up before being murdered?

Q4 Who did Theudebert II succeed as king?

Q5 What daughter of Theudebert II is said to have married Eadbald of Kent?

Q6 What was the name of Theudebert II's brother, with whom he was at war with for much of his life?

Q7 Ludegast was Bishop of what?

Q8 In what year did Theudebert II die?

Q9 What cousin did Theudebert II fight with his brother?

Q10 What territory was Theudebert II forced to cede to his brother in 610?

Theuderic II

Q1 Theuderic II became King of what after his father's death?

Q2 Theuderic II's wife Ermenberga was the daughter of which Visigoth king?

Q3 Who succeeded Theuderic II as king?

Q4 During his minority Theuderic II ruled under the guidance of which relative?

Q5 Who was Theuderic II's elder brother?

Q6 What is Theuderic II believed to have died from?

Q7 In what years did Theuderic II serve as King of Austrasia?

Q8 What position did Berthoald hold?

Q9 What bishop is said to have beseeched Theuderic II to spare his brother's life?

Q10 Where did Theuderic II die?

Sigebert II

Q1 How old was Sigebert II when he died?

Q2 What two kingdoms did Sigebert II inherit from his father?

Q3 Who succeeded Sigebert II as king?

Q4 How was Brunhilda related to Sigebert II?

Q5 Who was mayor of the palace of Burgundy during Sigebert II's reign?

Q6 In what year did Sigebert II reign?

Q7 Sigebert II was the bastard son of what king?

Q8 How did Sigebert II die?

Q9 By what river did Sigebert II's forces clash with those of the King of Neustria?

Q10 Who was Sigebert II's younger brother?

Chilperic I

Q1 Who was Chilperic I's mother?

Q2 Who was Chilperic I's eldest son?

Q3 Which of Chilperic I's wives were murdered?

Q4 What chronicler called Chilperic I 'the Nero and Herod of his time'?

Q5 In what year was Chilperic I assassinated?

Q6 Where was Chilperic I's kingdom based?

Q7 Who succeeded Chilperic I as king?

Q8 How many times did Chilperic I marry?

Q9 Who wrote the music for the operetta *Chilpéric*?

Q10 Chilperic I attempted to reform which alphabet?

Chlothar II (easy)

Q1 In what year did Chlothar II become King of the Franks?

A 589
B 602
C 613
D 624

Q2 Who was Chlothar II's mother?

A Fredegund
B Audovera
C Galswintha
D Sichilde

Q3 What royal house was Chlothar II a member of?

A Capet
B Valois
C Bourbon
D Merovingian

Q4 Chlothar II was known as the what?

A Tall
B Young
C Mean
D Bastard

Q5 Chlothar II became King of what in 584?

A Paris
B Orléans
C Neustria
D Burgundy

Q6 What famous edict was issued by Chlothar II around the year 614?

A Edict of Toulouse
B Edict of Rheims
C Edict of Paris
D Edict of Bruges

Q7 What son of Chlothar II became King of Austrasia in 623?

A Dagobert I
B Chilperic I
C Sigibert II
D Charibert II

Q8 How many times did Chlothar II marry?

A 0
B 1
C 2
D 3

Q9 What relative ran Chlothar II's kingdom in his minority?

A Half-brother
B Mother
C Uncle
D Great-grandfather

Q10 What relative was Chlothar II named after?

A Father
B Grandfather
C Great-great-great-grandfather
D Adoptive father

Chlothar II (expert)

Q1 Who was Chlothar II's father?

Q2 What Bishop of Rouen is believed to have been assassinated on Chlothar II's mother's orders?

Q3 Who became King of Aquitaine after Chlothar II's death?

Q4 Chlothar II was defeated at Dormelles in 599 by which two relatives?

Q5 In what year was Brunhilda executed?

Q6 Unlike most of his predecessors, what Christian practice did Chlothar II adhere to?

Q7 Before Chlothar II, who was the only Merovingian king to reign longer?

Q8 In what year did Chlothar II die?

Q9 How were Dagobert I and Charibert II related?

Q10 Saint Arnulf was Bishop of what?

Dagobert I

Q1 Where was Dagobert I buried?

Q2 Dagobert I's father made him King of what in 623?

Q3 What ruler did Dagobert I fight at the Battle of Wogastisburg?

Q4 What position did Pepin of Landen hold?

Q5 How was Sigebert III related to Dagobert I?

Q6 Dagobert I is said to have built what German castle during his reign?

Q7 Which of Dagobert I's wives died in 642?

Q8 Who was Dagobert I's father?

Q9 Dagobert I died near which city?

Q10 At the height of his power, what title did Dagobert I hold?

Clovis II

Q1 Clovis II succeeded his father as King of what?

Q2 Who succeeded Clovis II?

Q3 In what year did Clovis II become King?

Q4 Who was Clovis II's wife?

Q5 Who became mayor of the palace of Neustria in 641?

Q6 In what city was Clovis II buried?

Q7 *Roi fainéant* is a French term meaning what?

Q8 When Clovis II came to the throne, who acted as regent?

Q9 How many of Clovis II's sons went on to become kings?

Q10 What happened to Clovis II's wife as a young girl?

Chlothar III

Q1 After Chlothar III's death, who succeeded him as king?

Q2 What was Chlothar III king of from 658 until his death?

Q3 Who was Chlothar III's mother?

Q4 Audoin was Bishop of what?

Q5 What epidemic is reported to have struck during Chlothar III's reign?

Q6 Who succeeded Chlothar III as King of Austrasia?

Q7 How many brothers did Chlothar III have?

Q8 In what year did Chlothar III die?

Q9 What type of text was the *Liber Historiae Francorum*?

Q10 What position did Ebroin hold?

Childeric II

Q1 Childeric II was King of what for the last two years of his life?

Q2 Who was Childeric II's father?

Q3 In what year was Childeric II murdered?

Q4 What mayor of the palace dominated Childeric II's minority rule?

Q5 Where was Childeric II buried?

Q6 What relatives were murdered along with Childeric II?

Q7 How was Bilichild related to Childeric II?

Q8 What Bishop of Autun (who later became a saint) served during Childeric II's reign?

Q9 Childeric II became King of what in 662?

Q10 How was Childeric II related to his wife?

Theuderic III

Q1 Who did Theuderic III succeed as king in 673?

Q2 The Battle of Lucofao was fought against what kingdom?

Q3 In what years did Theuderic III serve as King of the Franks?

Q4 What important battle is reported to have taken place in 687?

Q5 Which relative succeeded Theuderic III as King of the Franks?

Q6 Which saint was a wife of Theuderic III?

Q7 Who ruled Austrasia before Theuderic III?

Q8 Who briefly deposed Theuderic III as King of Neustria and Burgundy?

Q9 On how many occasions did Ebroin serve as mayor of the palace of Neustria?

Q10 What was Pepin of Herstal's regnal number?

Clovis IV

Q1 Clovis IV served as King of what?

Q2 Who did Clovis IV succeed as king?

Q3 How was Pepin of Herstal related to Clovis IV?

Q4 Why is Clovis IV sometimes referred to as Clovis III?

Q5 Who was mayor of the palace during Clovis IV's reign?

Q6 As a puppet king, what French term was attributed to Clovis IV?

Q7 Who was Clovis IV's brother?

Q8 How was Clotilda related to Clovis IV?

Q9 In what century did Clovis IV rule?

Q10 How many children did Clovis IV have with his wife Tanaquille?

Childebert III

Q1 How was Childebert III's successor related to him?

Q2 Childebert III was nicknamed the what?

Q3 Who served as mayor of the palace during Childebert III's reign?

Q4 What were the Arnulfings?

Q5 In what year did Childebert III die?

Q6 Saint Aubert is said to have founded the monastery of what during Childebert III's reign?

Q7 How was Childebert III related to Charlemagne?

Q8 Who was Childebert III's father?

Q9 How many full brothers did Theuderic III have?

Q10 Where is Childebert III believed to have died?

Dagobert III

Q1 Dagobert III was King of what?

Q2 In what year did Pepin of Herstal die?

Q3 How was Theuderic IV related to Dagobert III?

Q4 What title did Savaric hold?

Q5 What relative did Dagobert III succeed as king?

Q6 In what years did Dagobert III's reign take place?

Q7 Dagobert III died before reaching what?

Q8 Who succeeded Pepin of Herstal as Duke of the Franks?

Q9 Who wrote the *Liber Historiae Francorum*?

Q10 What royal house was Dagobert III a member of?

Chilperic II

Q1 Before becoming a king, what name was Chilperic II known by?

Q2 Before he became King of the Franks, what title did Chilperic II hold?

Q3 Where was Chilperic II sent as an infant?

Q4 Chilperic II became a king after whose death?

Q5 Who succeeded Ragenfrid as mayor of the palace of Neustria?

Q6 Who did Chilperic II fight at the Battle of Vincy?

Q7 Who succeeded Chilperic II as King of the Franks?

Q8 Who was Chilperic II's father?

Q9 What king might have been the son of Chilperic II?

Q10 Whose death led to Chilperic II becoming King of the Franks?

Theuderic IV

Q1 Who was mayor of the palace during Theuderic IV's reign?

Q2 In what year did Theuderic IV die?

Q3 After Theuderic IV, how many more kings were there from the Merovingian dynasty?

Q4 Who was Theuderic IV's father?

Q5 In what year did Theuderic IV become king?

Q6 Theuderic IV was King of what?

Q7 Theuderic IV was what type of king?

Q8 Theuderic IV was held in custody in what abbey?

Q9 After Theuderic IV's death the throne remained vacant for several years until who became king?

Q10 What king might have been Theuderic IV's son?

Childeric III

Q1 Childeric III was the last king from what dynasty?

Q2 Who succeeded Childeric III as king?

Q3 In what year was Childeric III deposed?

Q4 Who was pope at the time of Childeric III's deposition?

Q5 What was done to Childeric III's body after his deposition?

Q6 How was Theuderic related to Childeric III?

Q7 Who painted *The Last of the Merovingians*?

Q8 Who was the eldest son of Charles Martel?

Q9 What political position was most powerful during Childeric III's reign?

Q10 Where was the Abbey of Saint Bertin located?

Pepin the Short (easy)

Q1 Pepin the Short was the first king from what dynasty?

A Merovingian
B Carolingian
C Valois
D Bourbon

Q2 In what year did Pepin the Short become king?

A 740
B 751
C 764
D 777

Q3 Pepin the Short was King of what?

A Burgundy
B The Franks
C Neustria
D Austrasia

Q4 How was Carloman related to Pepin the Short?

A Brother
B Father
C Uncle
D Cousin

Q5 What king did Pepin the Short have overthrown?

A Clovis IV
B Dagobert II
C Chlothar III
D Childeric III

Q6 Who was Pepin the Short's father?

A Charlemagne
B Carloman
C Charles Martel
D Gisela

Q7 What was Saint Boniface's birth name?

A Alfred
B Winfrid
C Drake
D Charles

Q8 The Donation of Pepin concerned what ruler?

A King of England
B Holy Roman Emperor
C Duke of Aquitaine
D Pope

Q9 What empire gave Pepin the Short the honorary title Patrician?

A Byzantine Empire
B Persian Empire
C Ottoman Empire
D Holy Roman Empire

Q10 How was Pepin the Short related to Charlemagne?

A Father
B Grandfather
C Uncle
D Nephew

Pepin the Short (expert)

Q1 Pepin the Short became sole ruler of the Franks after his brother retired where?

Q2 The Donation of Pepin concerned what pope?

Q3 What territory, under the direct rule of the pope, was established during Pepin the Short's reign?

Q4 In what year did Pepin the Short die?

Q5 Who was Pepin the Short's mother?

Q6 Where was Pepin the Short buried?

Q7 Who was Pepin the Short's wife?

Q8 Aistulf was the King of what group?

Q9 Pepin the Short fought against what Islamic state?

Q10 After his death, who was Pepin the Short's kingdom divided between?

Carloman I

Q1 Who was Carloman I's elder brother?

Q2 In what years did Carloman I's reign take place?

Q3 How was Gerberga related to Carloman I?

Q4 Who was the pope during Carloman I's reign?

Q5 What dynasty was Carloman I a part of?

Q6 Who was Carloman I's mother?

Q7 How old was Carloman I when he died?

Q8 What title did Carloman I share with his elder brother?

Q9 Where was Carloman I originally buried?

Q10 Where served as the capital of Carloman I's kingdom after his father's death?

Charlemagne (easy)

Q1 Charlemagne was known by what other name?

A Caleb
B Christopher
C Charles
D Cameron

Q2 Charlemagne was the first person to hold what title?

A King of France
B Holy Roman Emperor
C Byzantine Emperor
D King of Spain

Q3 What empire did Charlemagne establish?

A Carolingian Empire
B Byzantine Empire
C Angevin Empire
D Persian Empire

Q4 Who was Charlemagne's father?

A Desiderius
B Carloman I
C Pepin the Short
D Charles Martel

Q5 Charlemagne initially served as co-ruler with what relative?

A Father
B Brother
C Sister
D Uncle

Q6 *Capitulatio de partibus Saxoniae* was a legal code issued by Charlemagne as part of his determination to do what to the Saxons?

A Kill them
B Christianise them
C Pacify them
D Enslave them

Q7 What nickname was the eldest son of Charlemagne, Pepin, given?

A The Unready
B The Vain
C The Mad
D The Hunchback

Q8 In what year did Charlemagne die?

A 798
B 802
C 814
D 821

Q9 Some historians claim Charlemagne was…

A Homosexual
B Mad
C Born out of wedlock
D A cripple

Q10 Who was Charlemagne's second wife?

A Luitgard
B Fastrada
C Desiderata
D Hildegard

Charlemagne (average)

Q1 Charlemagne was known as The what?

Q2 Who was Charlemagne's mother?

Q3 The Massacre of Verden occurred during what series of wars?

Q4 Who crowned Charlemagne 'Emperor of the Romans'?

Q5 What relation succeeded Charlemagne?

Q6 Desiderata was the daughter of what king?

Q7 What siege took place between 773 and 774?

Q8 What crown was used in Charlemagne's coronation as King of the Lombards?

Q9 Charlemagne named his son, Louis, King of what in 781?

Q10 Where was Charlemagne buried?

Charlemagne (expert)

Q1 On what day of the year did Charlemagne become Holy Roman Emperor?

Q2 What renaissance started during Charlemagne's reign?

Q3 Charlemagne had his marriage to who annulled?

Q4 Which uncle did Charlemagne fight alongside during the Siege of Pavia?

Q5 What day of the year is Saint Angilbert's feast day?

Q6 The military leader Roland was killed in what battle?

Q7 The Karlsschrein was made on whose orders?

Q8 The epic poem *The Song of Roland* is based on what battle?

Q9 Where did Charlemagne's coronation as Holy Roman Emperor take place?

Q10 *Pax Nicephori* was a peace treaty between Charlemagne and what other ruler?

Louis the Pious

Q1 Who was Louis the Pious's mother?

Q2 Louis the Pious was King of what from 781?

Q3 What did Louis the Pious have done to his nephew, Bernard, which ultimately resulted in his death?

Q4 How many times did Louis the Pious marry?

Q5 Ebbo was Archbishop of what?

Q6 What pope crowned Louis the Pious Holy Roman Emperor?

Q7 In what year did Louis the Pious issue an imperial decree that laid out plans for an orderly succession?

Q8 The Treaty of Verdun divided the Carolingian Empire between how many of Louis the Pious's sons?

Q9 In what city was Louis the Pious buried?

Q10 In what year did Louis the Pious perform penance in public for the death of his nephew, Bernard?

Charles the Bald

Q1 In what year did Charles the Bald die?

Q2 Charles the Bald defeated Lothair I at what 841 battle?

Q3 The Oaths of Strasbourg were made by Charles the Bald and who else?

Q4 In what treaty did Charles the Bald and two of his brothers divide their father's kingdom?

Q5 Who did Charles the Bald fight at the Battle of Andernach (876)?

Q6 What book was presented to Charles the Bald in 846?

Q7 What group sacked Paris in 845?

Q8 In what year was the Battle of Jengland fought?

Q9 What important edict was issued in 864?

Q10 What was the nickname of Charles the Bald's eldest son, Louis?

Louis the Stammerer

Q1 Who was Louis the Stammerer's mother?

Q2 How was Charles the Child related to Louis the Stammerer?

Q3 What is Louis the Stammerer's regnal number?

Q4 Louis the Stammerer was King of what?

Q5 Which Archbishop of Rheims crowned Louis the Stammerer?

Q6 How old was Louis the Stammerer when he died?

Q7 After his death, Louis the Stammerer's kingdom was divided up between which two sons?

Q8 Who was Louis the Stammerer's first wife?

Q9 Where did Louis the Stammerer's coronation take place?

Q10 Which son of Louis the Stammerer was born after his death?

Louis III

Q1 In what years did Louis III reign?

Q2 Where was Louis III buried?

Q3 What poem celebrated the Battle of Saucourt?

Q4 Who was Louis III's younger brother?

Q5 How was Charles the Bald related to Louis III?

Q6 Where did Louis III's coronation take place?

Q7 In what year did the Battle of Saucourt take place?

Q8 Louis III signed what treaty with Louis the Younger in 880?

Q9 Louis III was King of what?

Q10 Louis III is believed to have been killed by hitting his head on what?

Carloman II

Q1 Carloman II was King of what?

Q2 Carloman II initially ruled with what relative?

Q3 In what year did Carloman II's coronation take place?

Q4 How was Carloman II related to his successor, Charles the Fat?

Q5 Boso renounced his allegiance to Carloman II after being elected King of what?

Q6 What was Carloman II said to have been doing when he died?

Q7 Who was Carloman II's mother?

Q8 In what year did Carloman II die?

Q9 Who painted a portrait of Carloman II and his brother in 1837?

Q10 Where is Carloman II buried?

Charles the Fat (easy)

Q1 What was Charles the Fat's regnal number?

A I
B II
C III
D IV

Q2 Who was Charles the Fat's father?

A Carloman II
B Charlemagne
C Louis the Pious
D Louis the German

Q3 In what year did Charles the Fat become Holy Roman Emperor?

A 870
B 881
C 892
D 901

Q4 Charles the Fat succeeded Carloman II as what?

A King of Paris
B King of West Francia
C King of the Franks
D Holy Roman Emperor

Q5 How was Louis the Younger related to Charles the Fat?

A Brother
B Cousin
C Nephew
D Uncle

Q6 What city faced a siege between 885 and 886?

A St Etienne
B Paris
C Marseille
D Vannes

Q7 Who was Charles the Fat's wife?

A Eadgyth
B Ageltrude
C Richardis
D Hemma

Q8 The *Annalista Saxo* is believed to have been written in what century?

A 9th
B 10th
C 12th
D 17th

Q9 Who preceded Charles the Fat as Holy Roman Emperor?

A Carloman II
B Louis the Younger
C Guy III of Spoleto
D Charles the Bald

Q10 Who was the leader of the Vikings during the Siege of Asselt?

A Harald Bluetooth
B Harald Hardrada
C Godfrid
D Erik the Red

Charles the Fat (expert)

Q1 Who crowned Charles the Fat Holy Roman Emperor?

Q2 What group were responsible for the Siege of Paris of 885–886?

Q3 What relative overthrew Charles the Fat shortly before his death?

Q4 In what year did Charles the Fat die?

Q5 Who was Charles the Fat's only son?

Q6 Charles the Fat accused the archchancellor, Liutward, of what?

Q7 In what present-day country was Charles the Fat buried?

Q8 What relative fled to Charles the Fat's court shortly before his deposition, seeking his protection?

Q9 Charles the Fat was the subject of what work of Latin prose, composed around the year 900?

Q10 Charles the Fat became King of what in 876?

Odo

Q1 What dynasty was Odo a part of?

Q2 Who was Odo's wife?

Q3 Before becoming a king, Odo was Count of what?

Q4 Who was Odo's father?

Q5 Odo's father was killed in what battle?

Q6 Odo fought in what siege that took place from 885-86?

Q7 How did Odo become king?

Q8 Where did Odo's coronation take place?

Q9 Walter was Archbishop of what between 887 and 923?

Q10 How was Odo related to his successor, Charles III?

Charles III

Q1 Charles III was nicknamed the what?

Q2 Charles III was a member of what dynasty?

Q3 Who was Charles III's father?

Q4 What treaty was agreed between Charles III and Rollo in 911?

Q5 How many times did Charles III marry?

Q6 Which son of Charles III went on to become a king?

Q7 Which King of England was Charles III's father in law?

Q8 Charles III became King of Lotharingia after whose death?

Q9 Who captured Charles III in 923?

Q10 The Treaty of Bonn was an agreement between Charles III and what other ruler?

Robert I

Q1 In what years did Robert I serve as king?

Q2 How was Robert I related to Odo?

Q3 Where did Robert I's coronation take place?

Q4 Robert I was killed in what battle?

Q5 How was Robert I's successor, Rudolph, related to him?

Q6 How was Beatrice of Vermandois related to Robert I?

Q7 Robert I's son was nicknamed the what?

Q8 Robert I was King of what?

Q9 Rollo was the first Duke of what?

Q10 Robert I was a member of what dynasty?

Rudolph

Q1 Rudolph served as King of what?

Q2 In what years did Rudolph serve as king?

Q3 Who conducted Rudolph's coronation ceremony?

Q4 Rudolph's brother, Hugh, was nicknamed the what?

Q5 Who was Rudolph's wife?

Q6 Rudolph's father was Duke of what?

Q7 Where did Rudolph's coronation take place?

Q8 What house was Rudolph a member of?

Q9 Arnulf I was the first Count of what?

Q10 Rudolph is often confused with what other ruler?

Louis IV

Q1 What does Louis IV's nickname *d'Outremer* mean?

Q2 Louis IV was the only son of what king?

Q3 How many half-sisters did Louis IV have?

Q4 After Louis IV's father was defeated in battle, where did he seek refuge with his mother?

Q5 Where did Louis IV's coronation take place?

Q6 Which of Louis IV's children became a queen?

Q7 Louis IV's wife, Gerberga of Saxony, was the sister of what king?

Q8 Who was Archbishop of Rheims when Louis IV became king?

Q9 Louis IV was a puppet of who for much of his reign?

Q10 In what year did the Synod of Ingelheim begin?

Lothair

Q1 In what years did Lothair serve as king?

Q2 Lothair was King of what?

Q3 Where was Lothair buried?

Q4 What present day country was Lothair's wife, Emma, from?

Q5 How was Bruno the Great related to Lothair?

Q6 How was Lothair's successor, Louis V, related to him?

Q7 What city was the place of Lothair's birth and death?

Q8 Who was the most powerful person in the kingdom when Lothair came to power?

Q9 What title did Lothair's brother, Charles, hold?

Q10 Where did Lothair attempt to capture the family of Otto II, Holy Roman Emperor in 978?

Louis V

Q1 Louis V was the last king from what dynasty?

Q2 Approximately how many years did Louis V's reign last?

Q3 What was Louis V's nickname?

Q4 How many children did Louis V have with his wife?

Q5 To the nearest five years, what was the approximate age difference between Louis V and his wife?

Q6 In what year did Louis V become co-king?

Q7 Who was Louis V's mother?

Q8 Louis V died while hunting in what forest?

Q9 Where did Louis V's coronation take place?

Q10 After Louis V's wife left him, who did she marry?

Hugh Capet

Q1 What royal house did Hugh Capet establish?

Q2 Who was Hugh Capet's father?

Q3 Where did Hugh Capet's coronation take place?

Q4 In what year was Hugh Capet elected king?

Q5 Hugh Capet removed what Archbishop of Reims from his position?

Q6 What position did Hugh Capet appoint his son, Robert II, to shortly after becoming king?

Q7 Hugh Capet was the King of what?

Q8 In what city did Hugh Capet die?

Q9 Hugh Capet appears in what famous work by Dante Alighieri?

Q10 Who was Hugh Capet's wife?

Robert II

Q1 Where was Robert II born?

Q2 How many marriages did Robert II have annulled?

Q3 In what years did Robert II reign as the sole ruler of the Franks?

Q4 Which pope excommunicated Robert II?

Q5 Who was Robert II's last wife?

Q6 What nickname was given to Robert II due to his devout Catholic beliefs?

Q7 Robert II reintroduced the custom of burning what sort of people at the stake?

Q8 Robert II confirmed the founding of what abbey in 1030-1031?

Q9 What three sons of Robert II rebelled against him?

Q10 Robert II served as co-king under who?

Henry I

Q1 Where was Henry I crowned co-king?

Q2 How old was Henry I when he died?

Q3 What title did Henry I give his brother, Robert I?

Q4 How was William the Conqueror related to Henry I?

Q5 What 1047 battle did Henry I and William the Conqueror fight against Guy of Burgundy?

Q6 Where did Henry I invade in 1054 and 1057?

Q7 Who served as regent after Henry I's death?

Q8 What siege was taking place when Henry I died?

Q9 Who was Henry I's first wife?

Q10 What title did Henry I's son, Hugh, hold?

Philip I

Q1 What was Philip I's nickname?

Q2 Who acted as regent in Philip I's minority?

Q3 What was unusual about Philip I's name at the time he was born?

Q4 Who did Philip I fight at the Battle of Cassel?

Q5 Who was the first person to excommunicate Philip I?

Q6 In what year was the Council of Clermont held?

Q7 Philip I's marriage to who resulted in him being excommunicated?

Q8 What crusade was launched during Philip I's reign?

Q9 Alberic was the first person to hold what position?

Q10 In what year did Philip I become co-king?

Louis VI (easy)

Q1 Louis VI was nicknamed the what?

A Bold
B Fat
C Hardy
D Jovial

Q2 How many years did Louis VI's reign last?

A 2
B 14
C 20
D 29

Q3 Where was Louis VI buried?

A Notre Dame
B Rheims Cathedral
C Chartres Cathedral
D Basilica of Saint-Denis

Q4 How many children did Louis VI have with his first wife, Lucienne de Rochefort?

A 0
B 1
C 4
D 12

Q5 Louis VI's second wife, Adelaide of Maurienne, was the niece of what pope?

A Sixtus II
B Gregory II
C Callixtus II
D Innocent II

Q6 Where did Louis VI's coronation take place?

A Orléans
B St Etienne
C Paris
D Rheims

Q7 Who was King of England when Louis VI came to the throne?

A William II
B Henry I
C Richard I
D Edward III

Q8 What kingdom did France fight in the Battle of Brémule?

A Denmark
B England
C Castile
D Hungary

Q9 Which Holy Roman Emperor launched an expedition against Louis VI in 1124?

A Conrad II
B Henry V
C Lothair III
D Frederick I

Q10 What civil war broke out in England shortly before Louis VI's death?

A The Anarchy
B The Wars of the Roses
C The English Civil War
D The Glorious Revolution

Louis VI (expert)

Q1 Who wrote *The Deeds of Louis the Fat*?

Q2 Who conducted Louis VI's coronation?

Q3 Which Count of Flanders was assassinated in 1127?

Q4 Shortly before his death, Louis VI was appointed as the guardian of what future Queen of France and England?

Q5 Who was Louis VI's mother?

Q6 How many members of the House of Capet had served as king before Louis VI?

Q7 What abbot, statesman and historian was a close advisor of Louis VI?

Q8 How many of Louis VI's sons served as king?

Q9 Who was Louis VI's youngest son?

Q10 In what year did Louis VI die?

Louis VII

Q1 Who did Louis VII's wife, Eleanor of Aquitaine, later marry?

Q2 What French university was founded during Louis VII's reign?

Q3 What crusade was fought during Louis VII's reign?

Q4 What famous Paris cathedral was built during Louis VII's reign?

Q5 Who was Louis VII's older brother?

Q6 What golden ornament did Pope Alexander III award Louis VII?

Q7 Which wife of Louis VII gave him a son and heir?

Q8 Where was Louis VII originally buried?

Q9 In what year did Louis VII's sole rule begin?

Q10 Which prominent friend and councillor of Louis VI also served under Louis VII?

Philip II (easy)

Q1 Philip II was first monarch to style himself as what?

A King of France
B King of the Franks
C Duke of Normandy
D Holy Roman Emperor

Q2 In what year did Philip II become junior king?

A 1143
B 1179
C 1190
D 1203

Q3 Philip II was known by what other name?

A Charlemagne
B The European
C Caesar
D Philip Augustus

Q4 Who was Philip II's mother?

A Eleanor of Aquitaine
B Adela of Champagne
C Marie of France
D Constance of Castile

Q5 Which chronicler wrote the *Gesta Philippi Augusti*?

A Petrus Comestor
B Thomas of Walsingham
C Rigord
D Jean Froissart

Q6 What war ended in 1214?

A Thirty Years' War
B Hundred Years' War
C Anglo-French War
D French Revolution

Q7 What empire did Philip II successfully break up?

A Angevin Empire
B Holy Roman Empire
C Byzantine Empire
D Austro-Hungarian Empire

Q8 What crusade was fought between 1209 and 1229?

A First Crusade
B Third Crusade
C People's Crusade
D Albigensian Crusade

Q9 How many times did Philip II marry?

A 1
B 2
C 3
D 4

Q10 How old was Philip II when he became sole king?

A 2
B 15
C 23
D 41

Philip II (expert)

Q1 What truce ended the Anglo-French War?

Q2 In what year was the Battle of Bouvines fought?

Q3 Philip II gave support to Robert Fitzwalter in what war that took place between 1215 and 1217?

Q4 What wall did Philip II have built around Paris?

Q5 Phillip II participated in the Third Crusade with which two other key European rulers?

Q6 How many of Philip II's children went on to serve as king?

Q7 What sister of Philip II was betrothed to Richard the Lionheart?

Q8 Philip II and who else signed the Treaty of Le Goulet?

Q9 Philip II appears in what William Shakespeare play?

Q10 Who wrote the *Battle of the Wines*?

Louis VIII

Q1 In what years did Louis VIII serve as King of France?

Q2 Who was Louis VIII's mother?

Q3 What was Louis VIII's nickname?

Q4 What kingdom did France fight against at the Battle of Roche-au-Moine?

Q5 How many times did Louis VIII marry?

Q6 Louis VIII was a pretender to what throne?

Q7 What did Louis VIII die from?

Q8 Where did Louis VIII's coronation take place?

Q9 What type of battle was the Battle of Sandwich?

Q10 The Battle of Lincoln was fought during what war?

Louis IX (easy)

Q1 Louis IX is commonly known by what name?

A Merlin
B Louis-Phillippe
C Louis Augustus
D Saint Louis

Q2 How old was Louis IX when he became king?

A 12
B 19
C 31
D 56

Q3 Who was Louis IX's mother?

A Isabella of Hainault
B Blanche of Castile
C Eleanor of Aquitaine
D Agnes of Merania

Q4 What crusade ended in 1229?

A The Third Crusade
B The Fourth Crusade
C The Albigensian Crusade
D The People's Crusade

Q5 What king did Louis IX face at the Battle of Taillebourg?

A Justinian I, Byzantine Emperor
B Henry III of England
C Christian II of Denmark
D Frederick I, Holy Roman Emperor

Q6 On what continent did Louis IX die?

A Africa
B Asia
C Europe
D North America

Q7 What church did Louis IX commission?

A Notre Dame
B Rheims Cathedral
C Sainte-Chapelle
D Sacré-Cœur

Q8 In what US state is a major city named after Louis IX?

A Arkansas
B Oklahoma
C Nebraska
D Missouri

Q9 Louis IX expanded what in the hope of eliminating heresy?

A The Reformation
B The Inquisition
C The Witch Trials
D The boundaries of the Kingdom of France

Q10 Geoffrey of Beaulieu served as what under Louis IX?

A Ambassador to Castile
B Mayor of the House
C Regent
D Confessor

Louis IX (expert)

Q1 What two crusades did Louis IX play an active part in?

Q2 Who wrote the *Life of Saint Louis*?

Q3 In what year did the Disputation of Paris take place?

Q4 Who was Louis IX's wife?

Q5 What did Louis IX die from?

Q6 In what present-day country was the Battle of Al Mansurah fought?

Q7 What happened to Louis IX at the Battle of Fariskur?

Q8 Louis IX is thought to have commissioned what bible?

Q9 Louis IV installed a house of what religious order at the Château de Fontainebleau?

Q10 In what years did Louis IX serve as King of France?

Philip III

Q1 What was Philip III's nickname?

Q2 What rebellion broke out on Sicily in 1282?

Q3 What favourite of Philip III was hanged in 1278?

Q4 What crusade did Philip III take part in?

Q5 Who was Philip III's second wife?

Q6 Where did Philip III die?

Q7 Mos Teutonicus was a custom relating to what?

Q8 The Treaty of Orléans was signed by Philip III and who else?

Q9 How was Charles I of Anjou related to Philip III?

Q10 In what year did Philip III become King of France?

Philip IV (easy)

Q1 What was Philip IV's nickname?

A The Devious
B The Fair
C The Great
D The Bold

Q2 As well as being King of France, Philip IV also served as King of what?

A Aragon
B Castile
C Navarre
D England

Q3 Bernard Saisset was Bishop of what?

A Orléans
B Saint-Étienne
C Pamiers
D Nice

Q4 What war did Philip IV take part in between 1297 and 1305?

A Franco-Flemish War
B War in the Vendée
C Franco-Prussian War
D French Wars of Religion

Q5 Where did Philip IV's coronation take place?

A Nice
B Paris
C Rheims
D Calais

Q6 From 1309 to 1376 seven successive popes resided in what city?

A Paris
B Avignon
C Rome
D Rheims

Q7 How many of Philip IV's sons went on to become King of France?

A 0
B 1
C 2
D 3

Q8 In what year did Philip IV become King of France?

A 1260
B 1274
C 1285
D 1301

Q9 Who defeated French forces at the Battle of the Golden Spurs?

A County of Flanders
B Papal States
C Duchy of Aquitaine
D Kingdom of England

Q10 What religious order did Philip IV have destroyed?

A Knights Hospitaller
B Knights Templar
C Teutonic Knights
D Order of the Holy Sepulchre

Philip IV (expert)

Q1 Which three daughters-in-law of Philip IV were involved in the Tour de Nesle affair?

Q2 What palace was Philip IV born in?

Q3 Who was Philip IV's wife?

Q4 What alliance was formed between France and Scotland in 1295?

Q5 The Treaty of Paris (1303) was signed by Philip IV and what other king?

Q6 In what year was the Battle of Mons-en-Pévèle fought?

Q7 What pope issued the papal bull *Unam sanctam*?

Q8 What daughter of Philip IV became Queen of England?

Q9 Which chief minister of Philip IV was executed a year after his death?

Q10 Philip IV considered forming an alliance with what empire in order to tackle Islamic influence in the Middle East?

Louis X

Q1 In what years did Louis X serve as King of France?

Q2 Louis X became King of what in 1305?

Q3 Who did Louis X marry the year before his death?

Q4 What was Louis X's first wife, Margaret of Burgundy, convicted of?

Q5 Louis X is reported to have died shortly after playing what sport?

Q6 The Tour de Nesle affair is believed to have largely occurred in what guard tower?

Q7 Louis X readmitted what persecuted group into France?

Q8 Who persuaded Louis X to have Enguerrand de Marigny executed?

Q9 Which of Louis X's children was born shortly after his death?

Q10 Who was Louis X's mother?

John I

Q1 What was John I's nickname?

Q2 How old was John I when he died?

Q3 Who served as regent during John I's reign?

Q4 Where was John I buried?

Q5 Who was John I's mother?

Q6 In what year was John I born?

Q7 How was Joan II of Navarre related to John I?

Q8 John I was the king of what two kingdoms?

Q9 *The Accursed Kings* is a series of historical novels written by who?

Q10 What royal house was John I a member of?

Philip V (easy)

Q1 What was Philip V's nickname?

A The Frail
B The Tall
C The Naïve
D The Pious

Q2 What position did Philip V hold during John I's reign?

A Mayor of Paris
B Archbishop of Rheims
C Co-king
D Regent

Q3 How was Philip V related to his predecessor, John I?

A Father
B Brother
C Cousin
D Uncle

Q4 What popular crusade was launched in 1320?

A The People's Crusade
B The Shepherds' Crusade
C Livonian Crusade
D Wendish Crusade

Q5 How was Philip V's successor, Charles IV, related to him?

A Cousin
B Brother
C Son
D Not related

Q6 Who was Philip V's wife?

A Mahaut, Countess of Artois
B Eleanor of Aquitaine
C Margaret of Anjou
D Joan II, Countess of Burgundy

Q7 What was Philip V's regnal number as King of Navarre?

A I
B II
C IV
D V

Q8 Under what law were women excluded from inheriting the throne?

A Charlemagne's law
B Gaul law
C Salic law
D Catholic law

Q9 Who was Philip V's eldest daughter?

A Blanche of France
B Margaret I, Countess of Burgundy
C Isabella of France, Dauphine of Viennois
D Joan III, Countess of Burgundy

Q10 In 1321 there was an alleged plot by what group to poison water supplies in France?

A Muslims
B Jews
C Lepers
D Huguenots

Philip V (expert)

Q1 What woman was a contestant for the throne when Philip V became king?

Q2 In what years did Philip V serve as King of France?

Q3 Who was Philip V's father-in-law?

Q4 What scandal was Philip V's wife accused of helping to cover up?

Q5 Who did Philip V's daughter, Margaret I, marry?

Q6 Edward II of England was supposed to pay homage to Philip V due to him being the ruler of what territory?

Q7 Who was Philip V's father?

Q8 Philip V played a key role in the development of what court?

Q9 What group was a popular crusade launched against in 1320?

Q10 Who was pope during Philip V's reign?

Charles IV

Q1 Charles IV was the last king from what royal house?

Q2 What nickname was Charles IV given in France?

Q3 Where did a peasant revolt take place between 1323 and 1328?

Q4 What ruler did Charles IV fight against in the War of Saint-Sardos?

Q5 How was Charles IV related to his successor, Philip VI?

Q6 What child of Charles IV was born after his death?

Q7 What title did Charles IV's nephew, also called Charles IV, hold?

Q8 Which of Charles IV's wives was imprisoned?

Q9 Charles IV died at what fortress?

Q10 Which uncle of Charles IV was a key advisor to the king in the first half of his reign?

Philip VI

Q1 What was Philip VI's nickname?

Q2 What royal house was Philip VI a member of?

Q3 What King of England claimed the French crown was rightfully his?

Q4 What prolonged war between England and France broke out in 1337?

Q5 What major naval defeat did Philip VI suffer in 1340?

Q6 What major pandemic struck France during Philip VI's reign?

Q7 In what year was the Battle of Crécy fought?

Q8 Philip VI purchased Dauphiné from what ruler?

Q9 What nickname was given to Philip VI's wife, Joan of Burgundy?

Q10 Philip VI served as King of France for just over how many years?

John II

Q1 What was John II's nickname?

Q2 What popular revolt took place in 1358?

Q3 John II was captured in what 1356 battle?

Q4 In what country was John II held captive?

Q5 The Treaty of Brétigny was signed by John II and what other king?

Q6 In what palace did John II die?

Q7 What position was Charles de La Cerda appointed to shortly after John II became king?

Q8 The Treaty of Valognes was signed by John II and who else?

Q9 In what years did the Siege of Calais take place?

Q10 Which wife of John II served as Queen of France?

Charles V (easy)

Q1 Charles V became Regent of France after what 1356 battle?

A Battle of Poitiers
B Battle of Crécy
C Battle of Sluys
D Battle of Caen

Q2 What was Charles V's nickname?

A The Francophile
B The Frugal
C The Mad
D The Wise

Q3 In what year did Charles V become King of France?

A 1364
B 1371
C 1379
D 1390

Q4 Who was Charles V's wife?

A Isabella of Valois
B Valentina Visconti
C Joanna of Bourbon
D Catherine of France

Q5 In what city did the Harelle revolt occur?

A Paris
B Calais
C Rouen
D Rheims

Q6 In what year did the Western Schism begin?

A 1360
B 1378
C 1393
D 1401

Q7 What war broke out in 1341?

A War of Spanish Succession
B War of the Breton Succession
C The Hundred Years' War
D Hussite Wars

Q8 What treaty did France and England sign in 1359?

A Treaty of London
B Treaty of Calais
C Treaty of Paris
D Treaty of Versailles

Q9 In what cathedral did Charles V's coronation take place?

A Notre Dame
B Rheims Cathedral
C Chartres Cathedral
D Bourges Cathedral

Q10 How was Charles V's successor, Charles VI, related to him?

A Son
B Grandson
C Brother
D Not related

Charles V (expert)

Q1 What group did Étienne Marcel represent?

Q2 The Great Ordinance of 1357 was an attempt to impose limits on what?

Q3 What knight was known as the Black Dog of Brocéliande?

Q4 The Battle of Cocherel was fought between France and what other kingdom?

Q5 Who led English forces at the Battle of Pontvallain?

Q6 Pope Gregory XI was the last pope to reside where?

Q7 Clement VII became what in 1378?

Q8 What was Christine de Pizan's occupation?

Q9 Who was Charles V's mother?

Q10 Charles V died at what royal castle?

Charles VI (easy)

Q1 What was Charles VI's nickname?

A The Cursed
B The Mute
C The Mad
D The Affable

Q2 How many years did Charles VI serve as King of France?

A 2
B 8
C 34
D 42

Q3 Who was Charles VI's wife?

A Joan, Duchess of Brittany
B Isabella of Brittany
C Isabeau of Bavaria
D Margaret of Anjou

Q4 Charles VI suffered from bouts of what?

A Paranoia
B Forgetfulness
C Insanity
D Anger

Q5 Which sibling of Charles VI was assassinated in 1407?

A Catherine of France
B Joanna
C John
D Louis I, Duke of Orléans

Q6 In what year did the Armagnac–Burgundian Civil War break out?

A 1376
B 1390
C 1400
D 1407

Q7 What was the final phase of the Hundred Years' War?

A Yorkist War
B Lancastrian War
C Anglo-French War
D Valois War

Q8 John the Fearless was Duke of what?

A Burgundy
B Orléans
C Aquitaine
D Normandy

Q9 The Treaty of Troyes was an agreement between Charles VI and which English king?

A Edward II
B Edward III
C Henry V
D Henry VI

Q10 What was the *Bal des Ardents*?

A Masquerade ball
B Meeting of European ambassadors
C Revolution
D Period of economic decline

Charles VI (expert)

Q1 How old was Charles VI when he became King of France?

Q2 What two factions took part in the Armagnac–Burgundian Civil War?

Q3 After Charles VI agreed to disinherit his offspring, who became heir apparent to the French throne?

Q4 Who was Charles VI's mother?

Q5 What royal residence was Charles VI born at?

Q6 What Flemish patriot was killed at the Battle of Roosebeke?

Q7 Who wrote the *Chronique de Religieux de Saint-Denys, contenant le regne de Charles VI de 1380 a 1422*?

Q8 Who was the first husband of Charles VI's daughter, Isabella of Valois?

Q9 In what year was the Battle of Agincourt fought?

Q10 What delusion did Charles VI suffer from?

Henry VI of England (easy)

Q1 Where was Henry VI crowned King of France?

A Chartres Cathedral
B Bourges Cathedral
C Westminster Abbey
D Notre Dame

Q2 How many children did Henry VI have?

A 0
B 1
C 3
D 8

Q3 Which church was Henry VI a member of?

A Anglican
B Catholic
C Methodist
D Orthodox

Q4 How was Joan of Arc executed?

A Stoned
B Hung, drawn and quartered
C Burned at the stake
D Guillotined

Q5 Which civil war broke out during Henry VI's reign?

A The Anarchy
B The Glorious Revolution
C The English Civil War
D The Wars of the Roses

Q6 Which royal house was Henry VI a member of?

A York
B Lancaster
C Blois
D Orange-Nassau

Q7 William Shakespeare's *Henry VI* consists of how many plays?

A 1
B 2
C 3
D 4

Q8 Henry VI suffered from bouts of what?

A Depression
B Paranoia
C Madness
D Rage

Q9 Where was William de la Pole executed?

A Tower of London
B Pontefract Castle
C Tyburn
D English Channel

Q10 The Loveday of 1458 took place at what cathedral?

A St Paul's Cathedral
B Winchester Cathedral
C Salisbury Cathedral
D Leicester Cathedral

Henry VI of England (average)

Q1 Who was Henry VI's wife?

Q2 Where did Henry VI die?

Q3 On how many occasions did Henry VI serve as King of England?

Q4 Where was Henry VI crowned King of England?

Q5 What was the name of Henry VI's heir?

Q6 Henry VI was liberated from his state of imprisonment in which 1461 battle?

Q7 Henry VI is buried in what castle?

Q8 Who paid the ransom for Margaret of Anjou's release in 1475?

Q9 How old was Henry VI when he became King of England?

Q10 What long-lasting war ended during Henry VI's reign?

Henry VI of England (expert)

Q1 Which three educational establishments did Henry VI establish?

Q2 What was Joan of Arc's nickname?

Q3 Who was declared Regent of France following the death of Henry V?

Q4 The Congress of Arras was held in what year?

Q5 The favourite of Henry VI, William de la Pole, was Duke of what?

Q6 Jack Cade's Rebellion occurred in what year?

Q7 The Readeption refers to what event?

Q8 Who is Margaret of Anjou buried next to?

Q9 At which 1460 battle was Henry VI captured?

Q10 What relation was Charles VI of France to Henry VI?

Charles VII

Q1 What faction supported the House of Valois in the Armagnac–Burgundian Civil War?

Q2 What prolonged war with England ended during Charles VII's reign?

Q3 What famous siege took place between 1428 and 1429?

Q4 How was Joan of Arc executed?

Q5 In what year was the Battle of Patay fought?

Q6 After the Battle of Castillon, England lost all its French possessions except for what?

Q7 Who also held a claim to the French throne during Charles VII's reign?

Q8 Representatives from France and what two other territories attended the Congress of Arras?

Q9 What notable figure was captured at the Siege of Compiègne?

Q10 What was Charles VII's nickname?

Louis XI (easy)

Q1 What was Louis XI's nickname?

A The Prudent
B The Dashing
C The Unworthy
D The Bold

Q2 In what year did Louis XI die?

A 1478
B 1483
C 1490
D 1500

Q3 What was the name of the rebellion Louis XI took part in against his father?

A The Praguerie
B The Peasants' Revolt
C The Glorious Revolution
D The Tyranny

Q4 Who served as Queen of France during Louis XI's reign?

A Marie of Anjou
B Margaret of Scotland
C Margaret of Anjou
D Charlotte of Savoy

Q5 How many times did Louis XI marry?

A 1
B 2
C 6
D 7

Q6 Louis XI and what English king signed the Treaty of Picquigny?

A Henry V
B Henry VI
C Edward IV
D Edward V

Q7 How many of Louis XI's sons went on to become King of France?

A 0
B 1
C 2
D 3

Q8 Who did the French fight at the Battle of St. Jakob an der Birs?

A Old Swiss Confederacy
B Papal States
C Holy Roman Empire
D Kingdom of England

Q9 Louis XI is buried near which French city?

A Bourges
B Rheims
C Orléans
D Paris

Q10 What daughter of Louis XI became regent shortly after his death?

A Louise of France
B Michelle of France
C Anne of France
D Joan of France

Louis XI (expert)

Q1 In what year was the Treaty of Picquigny signed?

Q2 What duke was killed during the Battle of Nancy?

Q3 What popular Victor Hugo novel is set during the reign of Louis XI?

Q4 What order of chivalry did Louis XI found in 1469?

Q5 What alliance of nobles was formed in 1465 in defiance of the centralised authority of Louis XI?

Q6 Louis XI was sometimes referred to as the Universal what?

Q7 What was the occupation of Jacques Cœur?

Q8 Before Louis XI became King of France, what title did he hold?

Q9 Louis XI's first wife, Margaret of Scotland, was a member of what royal house?

Q10 Where was Louis XI christened?

Charles VIII

Q1 What was Charles VIII's nickname?

Q2 How old was Charles VIII when he became King of France?

Q3 How did Charles VIII die?

Q4 Who was Charles VIII's wife, Anne of Brittany, betrothed to in 1480?

Q5 What war was fought between feudal lords and the French monarchy from 1485 to 1488?

Q6 What relative of Charles VIII acted as regent in the early stages of his reign?

Q7 What territory was united with France in 1491?

Q8 In what year did the First Italian War break out?

Q9 How was Charles VIII's successor, Louis XII, related to him?

Q10 What royal residence was Charles VIII born at?

Louis XII (easy)

Q1 Louis XII served as King of what between 1501 and 1504?

A Navarre
B Naples
C Castile
D Bohemia

Q2 Who was Louis XII's father?

A John the Fearless, Duke of Burgundy
B Charles, Duke of Orléans
C Richard III of England
D Charles VII of France

Q3 Who was Louis XII married to at the time of his death?

A Mary Tudor
B Henrietta Maria of France
C Marie of Cleves
D Lady Jane Grey

Q4 In what 1488 battle was Louis XII captured?

A Battle of Saint-Aubin-du-Cormier
B Battle of the Golden Spurs
C Battle of La Brossinière
D Battle of Formigny

Q5 What war did Louis XII take part in between 1494 and 1498?

A Wars of the Roses
B First Italian War
C Fifth Crusade
D War of Spanish Succession

Q6 What pope annulled Louis XII's first marriage?

A Pius VI
B Gregory VI
C Alexander VI
D Innocent VI

Q7 What duchy did Louis XII conquer in 1500?

A Normandy
B Burgundy
C Luxembourg
D Milan

Q8 Louis XII was proclaimed what in 1506?

A Holy Roman Emperor
B Father of the People
C Saint Louis
D A traitor

Q9 In what year did the War of the League of Cambrai break out?

A 1489
B 1496
C 1508
D 1523

Q10 What was Pierre Terrail's occupation?

A Playwright
B Merchant
C Knight
D Chronicler

Louis XII (expert)

Q1 Which wife of Louis XII became a saint?

Q2 In what years did the Second Italian War take place?

Q3 Where is the Tomb of Louis XII and Anne of Brittany located?

Q4 How was Louis XII related to his successor, Francis I?

Q5 In what year did Louis XII become King of France?

Q6 Louis XII featured in what famous work by Niccolò Machiavelli?

Q7 In what year was the Treaty of Granada signed?

Q8 Who did the French fight at the Battle of Agnadello?

Q9 What daughter of Louis XII served as Queen of France?

Q10 Who succeeded Louis XII as Duke of Milan?

Francis I (easy)

Q1 Who Francis I's father?

A Charles VIII of France
B Louis XII
C Charles, Count of Angoulême
D Charles, Duke of Orléans

Q2 How many times did Francis I marry?

A 0
B 2
C 4
D 6

Q3 Construction on what château started in 1519?

A Château d'Amboise
B Château de Chenonceau
C Château d'Ussé
D Château de Chambord

Q4 What famous painting did Francis I acquire?

A *The Starry Night*
B *Mona Lisa*
C *The Night Watch*
D *Guernica*

Q5 What was Jacques Cartier?

A Pretender to the French throne
B Chronicler
C Explorer
D Clergyman

Q6 Where was the Field of the Cloth of Gold located?

A Pale of Calais
B Paris
C Brussels
D St Etienne

Q7 Who was Sultan of the Ottoman Empire when the Franco-Ottoman alliance was formed?

A Selim I
B Suleiman I
C Bayezid II
D Murad III

Q8 In what town was Francis I born?

A Roscoff
B Quiberon
C Cognac
D Vannes

Q9 Who was Francis I's eldest son?

A Francis III, Duke of Brittany
B Henry II of France
C Francis II of France
D Charles II de Valois, Duke of Orléans

Q10 Francis I was a key patron of what?

A The arts
B Colonialism
C Ship building
D Science

Francis I (expert)

Q1 Who did Francis I meet at a summit on the Field of the Cloth of Gold in 1520?

Q2 Who was Francis I's first wife?

Q3 In what year did Francis I sign the Ordonnance de Montpellier?

Q4 The construction of what key administrative building in Paris began during Francis I's reign?

Q5 In what years did Francis I serve as King of France?

Q6 What ruler did Francis I fight against in the Italian War of 1536–1538?

Q7 New Angoulême was situated on the site of what present-day city?

Q8 In what year did the Siege of Nice take place?

Q9 The Affair of the Placards involved protests against what?

Q10 Francis I ordered a massacre in what village in 1545?

Henry II

Q1 Henry II died after doing what?

Q2 As a child, Henry II was held in captivity in what country?

Q3 What did the Peace of Cateau-Cambrésis end?

Q4 What territory did Henry II obtain from England?

Q5 In what years did Henry II serve as King of France?

Q6 What was Ambroise Paré's occupation?

Q7 The Edict of Châteaubriant imposed severe measures against what group of people?

Q8 What Scottish queen resided at Henry II's court?

Q9 How many children did Henry II have with his wife, Catherine de' Medici?

Q10 How many of Henry II's sons went on to serve as King of France?

Francis II

Q1 Who was Francis II's wife?

Q2 How old was Francis II when he died?

Q3 In what years did Francis II serve as King of France?

Q4 What was François Clouet's occupation?

Q5 As well as being King of France, what else was Francis II king of?

Q6 Who was Francis II's mother?

Q7 In what year was the Treaty of Edinburgh signed?

Q8 Who conducted Francis II's coronation?

Q9 The Amboise conspiracy was a failed attempt by what group to abduct Francis II?

Q10 Who plays Francis II in the TV series *Reign*?

Charles IX

Q1 How was Charles IX's successor, Henry III, related to him?

Q2 What group were the victims of the Massacre of Wassy?

Q3 In what year did the St. Bartholomew's Day massacre occur?

Q4 What French city was under siege between 1572 and 1573?

Q5 In what years did Charles IX serve as King of France?

Q6 What is Charles IX believed to have died from?

Q7 What war broke out in 1562?

Q8 In what year was the Edict of Boulogne signed?

Q9 The Battle of Saint-Denis was fought between what two groups?

Q10 Who was Charles IX's bastard son?

Henry III

Q1 Who was Henry III's father?

Q2 As well as being King of France, what other state did Henry III rule over?

Q3 In what year were the Henrician Articles adopted?

Q4 Who led the Malcontents during the Fifth French War of Religion (1574–1576)?

Q5 What three leaders were involved in the War of the Three Henrys?

Q6 Who assassinated Henry III?

Q7 Henry III was the last king from what royal house?

Q8 At what royal residence did Henry III die?

Q9 Who was named the Consul of France in Morocco?

Q10 What does the term *Les Mignons* refer to?

Henry IV (easy)

Q1 What was Henry IV's regnal number as King of Navarre?

A I
B II
C III
D IV

Q2 What was Henry IV's nickname?

A The Reformed
B The Great
C The Magnificent
D The Just

Q3 What royal house was Henry IV a member of?

A Bourbon
B Valois
C Capet
D Burgundy

Q4 How did Henry IV die?

A Jousting accident
B Dysentery
C In battle
D Assassinated

Q5 Who was Henry IV's father?

A Nicolas Henri, Duke of Orléans
B Charles IX of France
C Henry III of France
D Antoine of Navarre

Q6 What faith did Henry IV's mother, Jeanne d'Albret, adhere to?

A Catholic
B Protestant
C Orthodox
D None

Q7 What edict did Henry IV sign in 1598?

A Edict of Toulouse
B Edict of Calais
C Edict of Nantes
D Edict of Naples

Q8 Port-Royal served as the capital of what French colony?

A Acadia
B Louisiana
C French Guinea
D Guadeloupe

Q9 Who wrote *Henriade*?

A Alexis de Tocqueville
B Montesquieu
C Voltaire
D Jean-Jacques Rousseau

Q10 In what kingdom was Henry IV born?

A France
B England
C Navarre
D Bohemia

Henry IV (expert)

Q1 Who killed Henry IV?

Q2 Henry IV was a direct descendant of what saint and king?

Q3 Henry IV was celebrated in what song?

Q4 Henry IV's marriage to who was annulled?

Q5 In what years did Henry IV serve as King of France?

Q6 Where did Henry IV's coronation take place?

Q7 'Henry IV style' refers to a style of what?

Q8 The Peace of Vervins was signed by Henry IV and what other ruler?

Q9 Henry IV took part in a siege of what city in 1590?

Q10 The Battle of Ivry took place during what war?

Louis XIII

Q1 What was Louis XIII's regnal number as King of Navarre?

Q2 Who acted as regent during Louis XIII's minority?

Q3 What present-day country was Concino Concini from?

Q4 Who established the *Académie française* in 1635?

Q5 Louis XIII appears in what famous novel by Alexandre Dumas?

Q6 What favourite of Louis XIII was Duke of Luynes?

Q7 Who was Louis XIII's wife?

Q8 For what reason was Leonora Dori executed?

Q9 What major European war broke out in 1618?

Q10 The Treaty of Compiègne was a peace treaty between France and what other country?

Louis XIV (easy)

Q1 What was Louis XIV's nickname?

A The Old King
B The Patriotic King
C The Sun King
D The Holy King

Q2 Louis XIV reigned for just over how many years?

A 5
B 12
C 42
D 72

Q3 Louis XIV's personal rule began after whose death?

A Louis, Grand Dauphin
B Anne of Austria
C Cardinal Richelieu
D Cardinal Mazarin

Q4 What palace became the primary royal residence during Louis XIV's reign?

A Château de Fontainebleau
B Domaine National du Palais-Royal
C Luxembourg Palace
D Palace of Versailles

Q5 The Fronde was a series of what?

A Assassinations
B Civil wars
C Plague outbreaks
D Naval battles in the English Channel

Q6 The *Dragonnades* was a French government policy against what group?

A Jews
B Lepers
C Huguenots
D Peasants

Q7 A notable unidentified prisoner during Louis XIV's reign was said to have worn what?

A Feather hat
B Powdered wig
C Iron mask
D Golden boots

Q8 What war broke out in 1672?

A War of the League of Augsburg
B War of the Spanish Succession
C Franco-Dutch War
D War of Devolution

Q9 The War of the League of Augsburg was known by what other name?

A King Louis's War
B Nine Years' War
C German War
D War of Liberation

Q10 How many times did Louis XIV marry?

A 0
B 1
C 2
D 9

Louis XIV (average)

Q1 The War of the Spanish Succession was triggered by whose death?

Q2 In what present-day country was the Treaties of Nijmegen signed?

Q3 How was Louis XIV's successor, Louis XV, related to him?

Q4 Who was Louis XIV's mother?

Q5 In what city is the Hôtel national des Invalides based?

Q6 Style Louis XIV was a style of what?

Q7 Who was Louis XIV's first wife?

Q8 Which Spanish king signed the Peace of Utrecht?

Q9 In what present-day country was the Battle of Blenheim fought?

Q10 How many years after becoming King of France did Louis XIV's coronation take place?

Louis XIV (expert)

Q1 What countries were part of the Triple Alliance during the War of Devolution?

Q2 The Truce of Ratisbon ended what war?

Q3 In what year did Louis XIV's eldest son and heir, Louis, Grand Dauphin, die?

Q4 In what royal palace was Louis XIV born?

Q5 What order of chivalry did Louis XIV establish in 1693?

Q6 What treaty ended the War of Devolution?

Q7 In what year was the Battle of Oudenarde fought?

Q8 What North American colony was named in Louis XIV's honour?

Q9 In what war did the Siege of Namur (1695) take place?

Q10 How was Louise de La Vallière associated with Louis XIV?

Louis XV (easy)

Q1 What royal house was Louis XV a member of?

A Valois
B Bourbon
C Capet
D Burgundy

Q2 What was Louis XV's nickname?

A The Apostle
B The Frugal
C The Narcissistic
D The Beloved

Q3 How was Louis XV related to his predecessor, Louis XIV?

A Son
B Great-grandson
C Second cousin
D Not related

Q4 How old was Louis XV when he became King of France?

A 5
B 17
C 29
D 61

Q5 What position did André-Hercule de Fleury hold during Louis XV's reign?

A Archbishop of Rheims
B Co-king
C Chief Minister
D Regent

Q6 The Battle of Fontenoy was fought during what war?

A War of the Austrian Succession
B War of the Spanish Succession
C Nine Years' War
D Thirty Years' War

Q7 What two countries was New France ceded to?

A Germany and the United Kingdom
B Spain and Portugal
C Spain and the Netherlands
D Spain and the United Kingdom

Q8 What country did France fight in the Seven Years' War?

A Spain
B United Kingdom
C Portugal
D Sweden

Q9 How many of Louis XV's sons went on to serve as King of France?

A 0
B 1
C 2
D 4

Q10 Who was Louis XV's wife?

A Marie Adélaïde of Savoy
B Henriette of France
C Louise Élisabeth of France
D Marie Leszczyńska

Louis XV (average)

Q1 Who served as Regent of France in Louis XV's minority?

Q2 Who was the only French monarch to reign longer than Louis XV?

Q3 What became part of France in 1769?

Q4 What future French leader was born in 1769?

Q5 Who was the only son of Louis XV?

Q6 What present-day country was Louis XV's wife from?

Q7 What royal residence was Louis XV born at?

Q8 Louis XV's father was Duke of what?

Q9 The Battle of Rossbach was fought against what kingdom?

Q10 As well as being an economist, what was François Quesnay's occupation?

Louis XV (expert)

Q1 In what years did the Seven Years' War take place?

Q2 Who was Louis XV's mother?

Q3 Who was Louis XV's eldest daughter?

Q4 Rocaille was a style of what?

Q5 What type of battle was the Battle of Quiberon Bay?

Q6 The Treaty of Versailles (1756) was a diplomatic agreement between France and what other country?

Q7 In what year was the Battle of Minorca fought?

Q8 Who attempted to assassinate Louis XV in 1757?

Q9 The Battle of Fort Duquesne took place in what present-day US state?

Q10 In what years did Louis XV serve as King of France?

Louis XVI (easy)

Q1 By what name was Louis XVI referred to in the months before his death?

A He Who Shall Not Be Named
B Louis the Martyr
C Citizen Louis Capet
D The Bastard

Q2 In what year was Louis XVI executed?

A 1789
B 1793
C 1798
D 1801

Q3 What war broke out in 1789?

A Napoleonic Wars
B American Revolution
C Crimean War
D French Revolution

Q4 How was Louis XVI executed?

A Starved
B Firing squad
C Hung
D Guillotined

Q5 What present-day country was Louis XVI from?

A Austria
B Belgium
C France
D Italy

Q6 *Taille* was a tax on what?

A Alcohol
B Clothes
C Land
D Income

Q7 What was Anne Robert Jacques Turgot's occupation?

A Executioner
B Farmer
C Merchant
D Economist

Q8 The Treaty of Alliance (1778) was a defensive alliance between France and what other country?

A Spain
B USA
C United Kingdom
D Portugal

Q9 What political and social system ended under Louis XVI?

A *Ancien Régime*
B *Pax Francia*
C The Great Society
D The French Monopoly

Q10 How many Estates was the Estates General composed of?

A 2
B 3
C 4
D 5

Louis XVI (average)

Q1 Who was Louis XVI's wife?

Q2 Who was Louis XVI's executioner?

Q3 In what year was the Treaty of Paris signed, ending the American Revolutionary War?

Q4 What fortress was famously stormed in 1789?

Q5 What did the Third Estate form in 1789?

Q6 In what year did the Flight to Varennes occur?

Q7 After the fall of the French monarchy, what did the Kingdom of France change its name to?

Q8 What palace was stormed during the Insurrection of 10 August 1792?

Q9 Who was Louis XVI's eldest son?

Q10 Who was Louis XVI's mother?

Louis XVI (expert)

Q1 In what year did the Flour War take place?

Q2 Who was governor of the Bastille at the time it was stormed?

Q3 What was France's first written constitution?

Q4 Who was Louis XVI's only child to reach adulthood?

Q5 The Edict of Versailles was known by what other name?

Q6 What 1789 document did Thomas Jefferson help French revolutionaries to draft?

Q7 In what year did Louis XVI become King of France?

Q8 What Swedish nobleman was a close friend of Louis XVI's wife?

Q9 What adopted daughter of Louis XVI was born in 1778?

Q10 The Place de la Révolution, the site of Louis XVI's execution, is now known by what name?

Louis XVII

Q1 How old was Louis XVII when he died?

Q2 What title was Louis XVII given on his birth?

Q3 Where was Louis XVII born?

Q4 What was Louis XVII's birth name?

Q5 What part of Louis XVII's body was buried separately?

Q6 What was Antoine Simon's occupation?

Q7 Who was Louis XVII's older brother?

Q8 How was Louis XVII related to Louis XVI?

Q9 What was Alexander Kucharsky's occupation?

Q10 Where was Louis XVII imprisoned?

Napoléon Bonaparte (easy)

Q1 Where was Napoleon born?

A Corsica
B Sicily
C Majorca
D Barbados

Q2 What title did Napoleon adopt in 1804?

A King of the French
B President of France
C Emperor of the French
D Chief Minister

Q3 How many times did Napoleon marry?

A 0
B 2
C 4
D 5

Q4 How long did the Hundred Days last?

A 98 days
B 100 days
C 111 days
D 142 days

Q5 What empire did Napoleon establish?

A New Roman Empire
B First French Empire
C Napoleonic Empire
D Republican Empire

Q6 Napoleon led a military campaign in what country in 1798?

A United Kingdom
B Germany
C Spain
D Egypt

Q7 In what year did the Coup of 18 Brumaire take place?

A 1793
B 1799
C 1804
D 1815

Q8 How many coalitions were formed against Napoleon?

A 3
B 5
C 7
D 11

Q9 What empire was dissolved in 1806?

A Spanish Empire
B Austo-Hungarian Empire
C Ottoman Empire
D Holy Roman Empire

Q10 Who did the French fight at the Battle of Wagram?

A Kingdom of Prussia
B Austrian Empire
C Kingdom of Spain
D United Kingdom

Napoléon Bonaparte (average)

Q1 Where did Napoleon's coronation take place?

Q2 Which wife did Napoleon divorce?

Q3 What revolt did Napoleon help to suppress on 5 October 1795?

Q4 Before becoming Emperor, what title did Napoleon hold?

Q5 Who commanded British forces at the Battle of Waterloo?

Q6 In what year was the Battle of Austerlitz fought?

Q7 What army did Napoleon command during the Napoleonic Wars?

Q8 The Treaty of Tilsit followed Napoleon's victory in what battle?

Q9 Who did Napoleon install as King of Spain in 1808?

Q10 On what peninsula did the Peninsular War take place?

Napoléon Bonaparte (expert)

Q1 In what years were the Napoleonic Wars fought?

Q2 Who was the last Holy Roman Emperor?

Q3 What twin battles were fought on 14 October 1806?

Q4 What was the Continental System?

Q5 In what year did Napoleon invade Russia?

Q6 What two islands was Napoleon exiled to?

Q7 What royal dynasty was restored to power after Napoleon's defeat?

Q8 What civil code was established in 1804?

Q9 In what complex is Napoleon's tomb located?

Q10 Who was Napoleon's mother?

Louis XVIII (easy)

Q1 What was Louis XVIII's nickname?

A The Legitimate
B The Restored
C The Desired
D The Faithful

Q2 How was Louis XVIII related to Louis XVI?

A Brother
B Son
C Cousin
D Not related

Q3 What was Louis XVIII's title before he became King of France?

A Archbishop of Rheims
B Count of Provence
C Duke of Burgundy
D Dauphin of France

Q4 Who was Louis XVIII's wife?

A Marie Antoinette
B Marie Joséphine of Savoy
C Marie Thérèse of France
D No one

Q5 How many children did Louis XVIII have?

A 0
B 2
C 7
D 15

Q6 The Congress of what took place between 1814 and 1815?

A London
B Paris
C Madrid
D Vienna

Q7 In what year was Louis XVIII temporarily ousted?

A 1810
B 1813
C 1815
D 1819

Q8 What name is given to the period that followed Napoleon's defeat?

A New Era
B Bourbon Restoration
C *Ancien Régime*
D Constitutional Era

Q9 What was the Hundred Thousand Sons of Saint Louis?

A Royal succession
B An army
C A navy ship
D A book

Q10 In what present-day country was the Battle of Waterloo fought?

A Germany
B Italy
C Belgium
D Poland

Louis XVIII (expert)

Q1 How old was Louis XVIII when he died?

Q2 In what year did the Second White Terror take place?

Q3 What name was given to the first Chamber of Deputies elected after Louis XVIII's second restoration?

Q4 What was the Charter of 1814?

Q5 Who served as Louis XVIII's first Prime Minister?

Q6 After fleeing to England in 1807, what was the first house to become Louis XVIII's residence?

Q7 *Biens nationaux* refers to confiscated what?

Q8 What name was given to the period where Louis XVIII was temporarily overthrown by Napoleon?

Q9 How was Louis XVIII related to his successor, Charles X?

Q10 Where was Louis XVIII buried?

Napoleon II

Q1 In what year did Napoleon II serve as Emperor of the French?

Q2 Napoleon II was Duke of what?

Q3 Who was Napoleon II's mother?

Q4 In what palace did Napoleon II die?

Q5 How old was Napoleon II when he died?

Q6 What did Napoleon II die from?

Q7 Napoleon II became a cadet in what army?

Q8 How was Adam Albert von Neipperg related to Napoleon II?

Q9 How was Napoleon II related to Napoleon III?

Q10 In what year was Napoleon II born?

Charles X (easy)

Q1 Charles X was Count of what?

A Alsace
B Foix
C Artois
D Lorraine

Q2 How was Charles X related to Louis XVI?

A Son
B Grandson
C Brother
D Cousin

Q3 What did Charles X become after the Bourbon Restoration?

A A nationalist
B A republican
C A Protestant
D An ultra-royalist

Q4 Which child of Charles X was assassinated?

A Charles Ferdinand, Duke of Berry
B Louis Antoine, Duke of Angoulême
C Sophie d'Artois
D Marie Thérèse

Q5 Where did Charles X's coronation take place?

A Strasbourg
B London
C Rheims
D Paris

Q6 What was the Chamber of Deputies?

A A parliamentary body
B A diplomatic mission to the United Kingdom
C A privy council
D A guild

Q7 What country did France invade in 1830?

A Mexico
B United Kingdom
C Syria
D Algeria

Q8 What title did Jules de Polignac hold between 1829 and 1830?

A President
B Prime Minister
C Co-king
D Regent

Q9 What revolution resulted in Charles X's overthrow?

A Revolutions of 1848
B July Revolution
C French Revolution
D Glorious Revolution

Q10 In what present-day country did Charles X die?

A Russia
B United Kingdom
C France
D Italy

Charles X (expert)

Q1 Where was one of Charles X's sons assassinated?

Q2 What leader was defeated in the 1830 French legislative election?

Q3 In what years did Charles X serve as King of France?

Q4 Where is Charles X buried?

Q5 Who was Charles X's wife?

Q6 In what year were the July Ordinances issued?

Q7 What newspaper did Adolphe Thiers help to establish?

Q8 What grandson of Charles X was disputed King of France?

Q9 In what year was the Anti-Sacrilege Act passed?

Q10 In what year did Charles X die?

Louis Antoine

Q1 Approximately how long did Louis Antoine serve as King of France?

Q2 Louis Antoine was the last person to hold what title?

Q3 What was Louis Antoine's regnal number?

Q4 Louis Antoine was Duke of what?

Q5 What royal residence was Louis Antoine born at?

Q6 Who was Louis Antoine's wife?

Q7 How was Louis Antoine related to his predecessor, Charles X?

Q8 In what year did Louis Antoine die?

Q9 What relation did Louis Antoine abdicate in favour of?

Q10 What city did Louis Antoine settle in in late 1830?

Henri, Count of Chambord

Q1 What was Henri, Count of Chambord's regnal number?

Q2 Who was Henri, Count of Chambord's father?

Q3 What royal residence was Henri, Count of Chambord born in?

Q4 How was Henri, Count of Chambord related to Charles X?

Q5 What royal house was Henri, Count of Chambord a member of?

Q6 In what year did Henri, Count of Chambord disputably reign?

Q7 What were Henri, Count of Chambord's supporters called?

Q8 How many children did Henri, Count of Chambord have with his wife?

Q9 Who was Henri, Count of Chambord's mother?

Q10 What country did Henri, Count of Chambord die in?

Louis Philippe I (easy)

Q1 Who was Louis Philippe I's father?

A Henri, Count of Chambord
B Charles X of France
C Napoléon Bonaparte
D Louis Philippe II, Duke of Orléans

Q2 In what year was Louis Philippe I's father executed?

A 1789
B 1793
C 1801
D 1830

Q3 What royal house was Louis Philippe I a member of?

A Bourbon
B Napoleon
C Orléans
D Valois

Q4 Louis Philippe I was the last person to hold what title?

A Dauphin of France
B King of the French
C Emperor of the French
D Duke of Normandy

Q5 Who was Louis Philippe I's wife?

A Louise Marie Adélaïde de Bourbon, Duchess of Orléans
B Archduchess Maria Theresa of Austria-Este
C Maria Theresa of Savoy
D Maria Amalia of Naples and Sicily

Q6 Louis Philippe I was ousted during what revolution?

A French Revolution
B 1848 Revolution
C July Revolution
D Glorious Revolution

Q7 Louis Philippe I's reign was known as the what?

A Anarchy
B Great Restoration
C July Monarchy
D Treachery of 1830

Q8 What were Louis Philippe I's supporters known as?

A Orléanists
B Monarchists
C Legitimists
D Guardians of France

Q9 In what country did Louis Philippe I die?

A France
B England
C Sweden
D Italy

Q10 What royal residence was Louis Philippe I born at?

A Palace of Versailles
B Palais-Royal
C Luxembourg Palace
D Louvre Palace

Louis Philippe I (expert)

Q1 Who served as Prime Minister of France from 1847 to 1848?

Q2 Who was Louis Philippe I's eldest son?

Q3 In what years did Louis Philippe I serve as King of the French?

Q4 Louis Philippe I came to power after what revolution?

Q5 Where is Louis Philippe I buried?

Q6 Who attempted to assassinate Louis Philippe I in 1835?

Q7 How old was Louis Philippe I when he died?

Q8 Which English princess did Louis Philippe I propose to?

Q9 How many children did Louis Philippe I have with his wife?

Q10 What did the Kingdom of France become known as after Louis Philippe I's overthrow?

Napoleon III (easy)

Q1 How was Napoleon III related to Napoleon Bonaparte?

A Son
B Brother
C Cousin
D Nephew

Q2 Napoleon III was the first person to hold what title?

A Chancellor of France
B Emperor of the French
C President of France
D Prime Minister

Q3 Napoleon III came to power after what revolution?

A Peasants' Revolt
B French Revolution
C 1848 Revolution
D July Revolution

Q4 What empire did Napoleon III establish?

A First French Empire
B Second French Empire
C Third French Empire
D Fourth French Empire

Q5 What war took place between 1870 and 1871?

A Crimean War
B Franco-Prussian War
C Peninsular War
D First Boer War

Q6 What country did France fight against in the Crimean War?

A Russia
B United Kingdom
C USA
D Ottoman Empire

Q7 Napoleon III promoted the construction of what canal?

A Eerie Canal
B Panama Canal
C Briare Canal
D Suez Canal

Q8 The Cobden–Chevalier Treaty was an agreement between France and what other country?

A Italy
B Prussia
C Spain
D United Kingdom

Q9 What country did France intervene with in 1861?

A Canada
B Mexico
C Austria-Hungary
D Russia

Q10 In what year was Napoleon III overthrown?

A 1868
B 1870
C 1872
D 1880

Napoleon III (average)

Q1 In what years did Napoleon III serve as President of France?

Q2 Who directed a major public works program in Paris between 1853 and 1870?

Q3 Who became Emperor of Mexico in 1864?

Q4 Who served as the first Chancellor of Germany?

Q5 Napoleon III was captured during what battle?

Q6 What was proclaimed after Napoleon III's overthrow?

Q7 Who was Napoleon III's wife?

Q8 What country did Napoleon III move to after his overthrow?

Q9 Who was Napoleon III's father?

Q10 In what year did Napoleon III orchestrate a coup?

Napoleon III (expert)

Q1 What treaty ended the Franco-Prussian War?

Q2 Where is Napoleon III buried?

Q3 Who was Napoleon III's only child?

Q4 Who came second place in the 1848 French presidential election?

Q5 What treaty ended the Crimean War?

Q6 What telegram incited the French to declare war on Prussia?

Q7 What government ruled France between 1870 and 1871?

Q8 What architect did Napoleon III commission to restore Carcassonne?

Q9 What two major countries were unified around the time Napoleon III fell from power?

Q10 The Battle of Magenta was fought during what war?

Answers

Clovis I

Q1 The Franks
Q2 Merovingian dynasty
Q3 Childeric I
Q4 Syagrius
Q5 Catholicism
Q6 Saint Clotilde
Q7 481
Q8 Paris
Q9 Battle of Tolbiac
Q10 Sister

Theuderic I

Q1 Suavegotha
Q2 Theudebert I
Q3 3
Q4 *Beowulf*
Q5 Burgundy
Q6 Abbey of Saint-Pierre-le-Vif
Q7 Rheims
Q8 Childebert I
Q9 Hermanafrid
Q10 524

Theudebert I

Q1 His son, Theudebald
Q2 Gregory of Tours
Q3 Austrasian Letters
Q4 Hygelac
Q5 Justinian I
Q6 Coins bearing his own image
Q7 Wife
Q8 Gallo-Roman
Q9 His uncles, Childebert and Clotaire I
Q10 Merovingian dynasty

Theudebald

Q1 Waldrada
Q2 555
Q3 Father
Q4 Byzantine Empire
Q5 Wacho, King of the Lombards
Q6 Austrasia
Q7 Chlothar I
Q8 Ill health
Q9 General
Q10 5th-8th centuries

Chlodomer

Q1 Clovis I
Q2 Orléans
Q3 Battle of Vézeronce
Q4 524
Q5 3
Q6 Theuderic I, Childebert I and Clothar I
Q7 His brother, Clothar I
Q8 Sigismund of Burgundy
Q9 Saint Clodoald
Q10 His brother, Chlothar I

Childebert I

Q1 Rheims
Q2 Saint Clotilde
Q3 Paris
Q4 524
Q5 2
Q6 Sister
Q7 2
Q8 Christianity
Q9 His brother, Chlothar I
Q10 Ultragotha

Chlothar I

Q1 5
Q2 558
Q3 Soissons
Q4 Monogamy
Q5 His brother, Chlodomer
Q6 Ingund and Aregund
Q7 Nephew
Q8 Saint Clodoald
Q9 Royalty
Q10 Chram

Charibert I

Q1 Paris
Q2 Ingund
Q3 561
Q4 Wife
Q5 Bertha of Kent
Q6 Æthelberht of Kent
Q7 3
Q8 Excommunicated
Q9 Blavia castellum (a Roman military fort)
Q10 The realm was divided between his brothers

Guntram

Q1 Orléans
Q2 Chlothar I
Q3 561 to 592
Q4 Saint
Q5 Gregory of Tours
Q6 General
Q7 His nephew, Childebert II
Q8 Chlothar I
Q9 Fredegund
Q10 Chalon-sur-Saône

Sigebert I

Q1 Brunhilda
Q2 Austrasia
Q3 Pannonian Avars
Q4 Childebert II
Q5 The Visigoths
Q6 Half-brother
Q7 Assassination
Q8 Vitry-en-Artois
Q9 Chilperic I
Q10 561 to circa 575

Childebert II

Q1 Burgundy
Q2 Guntram
Q3 595
Q4 Assassination
Q5 Provence
Q6 587
Q7 Austrasia
Q8 Theuderic II and Theudebert II
Q9 Maurice, Emperor of the Byzantine Empire
Q10 Brunhilda

Theudebert II

Q1 Grandmother
Q2 Bilichildis
Q3 A monastery
Q4 His father, Childebert II
Q5 Emma of Austrasia
Q6 Theuderic II
Q7 Mainz
Q8 612
Q9 Chlothar II
Q10 Alsace

Theuderic II

Q1 Burgundy
Q2 Witteric
Q3 His illegitimate son, Sigebert II
Q4 His grandmother, Brunhilda
Q5 Theudebert II
Q6 Dysentery
Q7 612-13
Q8 Mayor of the palace of Burgundy
Q9 Ludegast, Bishop of Mainz
Q10 Metz

Sigebert II

Q1 12
Q2 Burgundy and Austrasia
Q3 Chlothar II
Q4 Great-grandmother
Q5 Warnachar II
Q6 613
Q7 Theuderic II
Q8 Executed
Q9 Aisne
Q10 Corbo / Corbus

Chilperic I

Q1 Aregund
Q2 Theudebert of Soissons
Q3 Galswintha
Q4 Gregory of Tours
Q5 584
Q6 Soissons
Q7 His son, Chlothar II
Q8 3
Q9 Hervé (Louis Auguste Florimond Ronger)
Q10 Frankish

<u>Chlothar II (easy)</u>

Q1 613
Q2 Fredegund
Q3 Merovingian
Q4 Young
Q5 Neustria
Q6 Edict of Paris
Q7 Dagobert I
Q8 3
Q9 Mother
Q10 Grandfather

<u>Chlothar II (expert)</u>

Q1 Chilperic I
Q2 Pretextatus
Q3 His son, Charibert II
Q4 His nephews, Theuderic II of Burgundy and Theudebert II of Austrasia
Q5 613
Q6 Monogamy
Q7 Chlothar I
Q8 629
Q9 Half-brothers
Q10 Metz

<u>Dagobert I</u>

Q1 Basilica of Saint-Denis
Q2 King of Austrasia
Q3 Samo
Q4 Mayor of the Palace of Austrasia
Q5 Son
Q6 Meersburg Castle
Q7 Nanthild
Q8 Chlothar II
Q9 Paris
Q10 King of the Franks

Clovis II

Q1 Neustria and Burgundy
Q2 His son, Chlothar III
Q3 639
Q4 Balthild
Q5 Erchinoald
Q6 Paris
Q7 Do-nothing king
Q8 His mother, Nanthild
Q9 3
Q10 Sold into slavery

Chlothar III

Q1 Theuderic III
Q2 Neustria and Burgundy
Q3 Balthild
Q4 Rouen
Q5 Plague
Q6 Childeric II
Q7 2
Q8 673
Q9 Chronicle
Q10 Mayor of the palace of Neustria

Childeric II

Q1 The Franks
Q2 Clovis II
Q3 675
Q4 Wulfoald
Q5 Saint-Germain-des-Prés
Q6 His wife, Bilichild and eldest son, Dagobert
Q7 Wife
Q8 Saint Leodegar
Q9 Austrasia
Q10 Cousin

Theuderic III

Q1 His brother, Chlothar III
Q2 Austrasia
Q3 679-691
Q4 Battle of Tertry
Q5 His son, Clovis IV
Q6 Saint Amalberga of Maubeuge
Q7 Dagobert II
Q8 Childeric II
Q9 2
Q10 II

Clovis IV

Q1 The Franks
Q2 His father, Theuderic III
Q3 Uncle
Q4 Because the other Clovis III was considered by some to be a usurper
Q5 Pepin of Herstal
Q6 *Roi fainéant* (Do-nothing king)
Q7 Childebert III
Q8 Mother
Q9 7th century
Q10 0

Childebert III

Q1 His son, Dagobert III
Q2 Just
Q3 Pepin of Herstal
Q4 An aristocratic family
Q5 711
Q6 Mont-Saint-Michel
Q7 Great-grandfather
Q8 Theuderic III
Q9 1
Q10 Saint-Étienne

Dagobert III

Q1 The Franks
Q2 714
Q3 Son
Q4 Bishop of Auxerre
Q5 His father, Childebert III
Q6 711-15
Q7 The age of majority
Q8 Charles Martel
Q9 Anonymous
Q10 Merovingian

Chilperic II

Q1 Daniel
Q2 King of Neustria
Q3 A monastery
Q4 Dagobert III
Q5 Charles Martel
Q6 Charles Martel
Q7 Theuderic IV
Q8 Childeric II
Q9 Childeric III
Q10 Chlothar IV

Theuderic IV

Q1 Charles Martel
Q2 737
Q3 1
Q4 Dagobert III
Q5 721
Q6 The Franks
Q7 Puppet
Q8 Chelles Abbey
Q9 Childeric III
Q10 Childeric III

Childeric III

Q1 Merovingian dynasty
Q2 Pepin the Short
Q3 751
Q4 Zachary
Q5 Tonsured
Q6 Son
Q7 Évariste Vital Luminais
Q8 Carloman
Q9 Mayor of the Palace
Q10 Saint-Omer

Pepin the Short (easy)

Q1 Carolingian
Q2 751
Q3 The Franks
Q4 Brother
Q5 Childeric III
Q6 Charles Martel
Q7 Winfrid
Q8 Pope
Q9 Byzantine Empire
Q10 Father

Pepin the Short (expert)

Q1 A monastery
Q2 Stephen II
Q3 Papal States
Q4 768
Q5 Rotrude
Q6 Basilica of Saint-Denis
Q7 Bertrada of Laon
Q8 Lombards
Q9 Umayyad Caliphate
Q10 His sons, Charlemagne and Carloman I

Carloman I

Q1 Charlemagne
Q2 768-771
Q3 Wife
Q4 Stephen III
Q5 Carolingian
Q6 Bertrada of Laon
Q7 20
Q8 King of the Franks
Q9 Rheims
Q10 Soissons

Charlemagne (easy)

Q1 Charles
Q2 Holy Roman Emperor
Q3 Carolingian Empire
Q4 Pepin the Short
Q5 Brother
Q6 Christianise them
Q7 The Hunchback
Q8 814
Q9 Born out of wedlock
Q10 Hildegard

Charlemagne (average)

Q1 Great
Q2 Bertrada of Laon
Q3 Saxon Wars
Q4 Pope Leo III
Q5 His son, Louis the Pious
Q6 Desiderius, King of the Lombards
Q7 Siege of Pavia
Q8 Iron Crown of Lombardy
Q9 Aquitaine
Q10 Aachen Cathedral

Charlemagne (expert)

Q1 25th December
Q2 Carolingian Renaissance
Q3 Desiderata
Q4 Bernard
Q5 18 February
Q6 Battle of Roncevaux Pass
Q7 Frederick II, Holy Roman Emperor
Q8 Battle of Roncevaux Pass
Q9 Old St. Peter's Basilica
Q10 Nikephoros I, Byzantine Emperor

Louis the Pious

Q1 Hildegard
Q2 Aquitaine
Q3 Blinded
Q4 2
Q5 Rheims
Q6 Pope Stephen IV
Q7 817
Q8 3
Q9 Metz
Q10 822

Charles the Bald

Q1 877
Q2 Battle of Fontenoy
Q3 Louis the German
Q4 Treaty of Verdun
Q5 Louis the Younger
Q6 *First Bible of Charles the Bald*
Q7 Vikings
Q8 851
Q9 Edict of Pistres
Q10 The Stammerer

Louis the Stammerer

Q1 Ermentrude of Orléans
Q2 Brother
Q3 II
Q4 West Francia
Q5 Hincmar
Q6 32
Q7 Carloman II and Louis III
Q8 Ansgarde of Burgundy
Q9 Compiègne
Q10 Charles the Simple

Louis III

Q1 879-82
Q2 Basilica of St Denis
Q3 *Ludwigslied*
Q4 Carloman II
Q5 Grandfather
Q6 Ferrières Abbey
Q7 881
Q8 Treaty of Ribemont
Q9 West Francia
Q10 A door lintel

Carloman II

Q1 West Francia
Q2 His brother, Louis III
Q3 879
Q4 Cousin
Q5 Provence
Q6 Hunting
Q7 Ansgarde of Burgundy
Q8 884
Q9 Charles de Steuben
Q10 Saint Denis Basilica

160

Charles the Fat (easy)

Q1 III
Q2 Louis the German
Q3 881
Q4 King of West Francia
Q5 Brother
Q6 Paris
Q7 Richardis
Q8 12th
Q9 Charles the Bald
Q10 Godfrid

Charles the Fat (expert)

Q1 Pope John VIII
Q2 Vikings
Q3 His nephew, Arnulf of Carinthia
Q4 888
Q5 Bernard
Q6 Having an affair with his wife
Q7 Germany
Q8 Louis the Blind
Q9 *Visio Karoli Grossi*
Q10 East Francia

Odo

Q1 Robertians
Q2 Théodrate of Troyes
Q3 Paris
Q4 Robert the Strong
Q5 Battle of Brissarthe
Q6 Siege of Paris
Q7 Elected by nobles
Q8 Compiègne
Q9 Sens
Q10 Not related

Charles III

Q1 Simple
Q2 Carolingian
Q3 Louis the Stammerer
Q4 Treaty of Saint-Clair-sur-Epte
Q5 2
Q6 Louis IV
Q7 Edward the Elder
Q8 Louis the Child, King of East Francia
Q9 Herbert II, Count of Vermandois
Q10 Henry the Fowler, King of East Francia

Robert I

Q1 922-23
Q2 Brother
Q3 Rheims
Q4 Battle of Soissons
Q5 Son in law
Q6 Wife
Q7 Great
Q8 West Francia
Q9 Normandy
Q10 Robertian

Rudolph

Q1 West Francia
Q2 923-36
Q3 Walter, Archbishop of Sens
Q4 Black
Q5 Emma of France
Q6 Burgundy
Q7 Soissons
Q8 Bivinids
Q9 Flanders
Q10 Rudolph I of Burgundy

Louis IV

Q1 From overseas
Q2 Charles the Simple
Q3 6
Q4 Wessex
Q5 Laon
Q6 Matilda, Queen of Burgundy
Q7 Otto I, Holy Roman Emperor
Q8 Artald
Q9 Hugh the Great
Q10 948

Lothair

Q1 954-86
Q2 West Francia
Q3 Abbey of Saint-Remi
Q4 Italy
Q5 Uncle
Q6 Son
Q7 Laon
Q8 Hugh the Great
Q9 Duke of Lower Lorraine
Q10 Aachen

Louis V

Q1 Carolingian
Q2 1
Q3 The Do-Nothing
Q4 0
Q5 25
Q6 979
Q7 Emma of Italy
Q8 Forest of Halatte
Q9 Compiègne
Q10 William I of Provence

Hugh Capet

Q1 House of Capet
Q2 Hugh the Great
Q3 Noyon
Q4 987
Q5 Arnulf
Q6 Co-king
Q7 The Franks
Q8 Paris
Q9 The *Divine Comedy*
Q10 Adelaide of Aquitaine

Robert II

Q1 Orléans
Q2 2
Q3 996-1031
Q4 Pope Gregory V
Q5 Constance of Arles
Q6 The Pious
Q7 Heretics
Q8 Noyers Abbey
Q9 Hugh Magnus, Henry I of France and Robert I of Burgundy
Q10 His father, Hugh Capet

Henry I

Q1 Rheims Cathedral
Q2 52
Q3 Duke of Burgundy
Q4 Nephew in law
Q5 The Battle of Val-ès-Dunes
Q6 Normandy
Q7 His wife, Anne of Kiev
Q8 Siege of Thimert
Q9 Matilda of Frisia
Q10 Count of Vermandois

Philip I

Q1 The Amorous
Q2 His mother, Anne of Kiev
Q3 It was of Greek origin
Q4 Robert I of Flanders
Q5 Hugh of Die
Q6 1095
Q7 Bertrade de Montfort
Q8 First Crusade
Q9 Grand Constable of France
Q10 1059

Louis VI (easy)

Q1 Fat
Q2 29
Q3 Basilica of Saint-Denis
Q4 0
Q5 Callixtus II
Q6 Orléans
Q7 Henry I
Q8 England
Q9 Henry V
Q10 The Anarchy

Louis VI (expert)

Q1 Suger
Q2 Daimbert, Archbishop of Sens
Q3 Charles the Good
Q4 Eleanor of Aquitaine
Q5 Bertha of Holland
Q6 4
Q7 Suger
Q8 2
Q9 Peter I of Courtenay
Q10 1137

Louis VII

Q1 Henry II of England
Q2 University of Paris
Q3 Second Crusade
Q4 Notre Dame
Q5 Philip of France
Q6 The Golden Rose
Q7 Adela of Champagne
Q8 Barbeau Abbey
Q9 1137
Q10 Suger

Philip II (easy)

Q1 King of France
Q2 1179
Q3 Philip Augustus
Q4 Adela of Champagne
Q5 Rigord
Q6 Anglo-French War
Q7 Angevin Empire
Q8 Albigensian Crusade
Q9 3
Q10 15

Philip II (expert)

Q1 Truce of Chinon
Q2 1214
Q3 First Barons' War
Q4 The Wall of Philip II Augustus
Q5 Richard I of England and Frederick I Barbarossa, Holy Roman Emperor
Q6 1
Q7 Alys of France, Countess of Vexin
Q8 King John of England
Q9 *The Life and Death of King John*
Q10 Henry d'Andeli

Louis VIII

Q1 1223-26
Q2 Isabelle of Hainaut
Q3 The Lion
Q4 England
Q5 1
Q6 Kingdom of England
Q7 Dysentery
Q8 Rheims
Q9 Naval battle
Q10 The First Barons' War

Louis IX (easy)

Q1 Saint Louis
Q2 12
Q3 Blanche of Castile
Q4 The Albigensian Crusade
Q5 Henry III of England
Q6 Africa
Q7 Sainte-Chapelle
Q8 Missouri
Q9 The Inquisition
Q10 Confessor

Louis IX (expert)

Q1 The Seventh Crusade and the Eighth Crusade
Q2 Jean de Joinville
Q3 1240
Q4 Margaret of Provence
Q5 Dysentery
Q6 Egypt
Q7 Captured
Q8 *Morgan Bible*
Q9 Trinitarian Order
Q10 1226-70

Philip III

Q1 The Bold
Q2 The Sicilian Vespers
Q3 Pierre de la Broce
Q4 Aragonese Crusade
Q5 Marie of Brabant
Q6 Perpignan
Q7 Funerals
Q8 Blanche of Artois
Q9 Uncle
Q10 1270

Philip IV (easy)

Q1 The Fair
Q2 Navarre
Q3 Pamiers
Q4 Franco-Flemish War
Q5 Rheims
Q6 Avignon
Q7 3
Q8 1285
Q9 County of Flanders
Q10 Knights Templar

Philip IV (expert)

Q1 Margaret of Burgundy, Blanche of Burgundy and Joan II, Countess of Burgundy
Q2 Palace of Fontainebleau
Q3 Joan I of Navarre
Q4 Auld Alliance
Q5 Edward I of England
Q6 1304
Q7 Boniface VIII
Q8 Isabella of France
Q9 Enguerrand de Marigny
Q10 Mongol Empire

Louis X

Q1 1314-16
Q2 Navarre
Q3 Clementia of Hungary
Q4 Adultery
Q5 Real tennis
Q6 Tour de Nesle
Q7 Jews
Q8 Charles, Count of Valois
Q9 John I
Q10 Joan I of Navarre

John I

Q1 The Posthumous
Q2 5 days
Q3 His uncle, Philip V
Q4 Basilica of Saint-Denis
Q5 Clementia of Hungary
Q6 1316
Q7 Half-sister
Q8 France and Navarre
Q9 Maurice Druon
Q10 House of Capet

Philip V (easy)

Q1 The Tall
Q2 Regent
Q3 Uncle
Q4 The Shepherds' Crusade
Q5 Brother
Q6 Joan II, Countess of Burgundy
Q7 II
Q8 Salic law
Q9 Joan III, Countess of Burgundy
Q10 Lepers

Philip V (expert)

Q1 Joan II of Navarre
Q2 1316-22
Q3 Otto IV, Count of Burgundy
Q4 Tour de Nesle affair
Q5 Louis I, Count of Flanders
Q6 Gascony
Q7 Philip IV of France
Q8 Court of Auditors
Q9 Moors
Q10 John XXII

Charles IV

Q1 House of Capet
Q2 The Fair
Q3 Flanders
Q4 Edward II of England
Q5 Cousin
Q6 Blanche of France, Duchess of Orléans
Q7 Holy Roman Emperor
Q8 Blanche of Burgundy
Q9 Château de Vincennes
Q10 Charles, Count of Valois

Philip VI

Q1 The Fortunate
Q2 House of Valois
Q3 Edward III of England
Q4 The Hundred Years' War
Q5 The Battle of Sluys
Q6 Black Death
Q7 1346
Q8 Humbert II, Dauphin of Viennois
Q9 Joan the Lame
Q10 22

John II

Q1 The Good
Q2 Jacquerie
Q3 Battle of Poitiers
Q4 England
Q5 Edward III of England
Q6 The Savoy Palace, London
Q7 Constable of France
Q8 Charles II of Navarre
Q9 1346–1347
Q10 Joan I, Countess of Auvergne

Charles V (easy)

Q1 Battle of Poitiers
Q2 The Wise
Q3 1364
Q4 Joanna of Bourbon
Q5 Rouen
Q6 1378
Q7 War of the Breton Succession
Q8 Treaty of London
Q9 Rheims Cathedral
Q10 Son

Charles V (expert)

Q1 Merchants
Q2 The power of the French monarchy
Q3 Bertrand du Guesclin
Q4 Navarre
Q5 Robert Knolles
Q6 Avignon
Q7 Antipope
Q8 Author
Q9 Bonne of Luxembourg
Q10 Beauté-sur-Marne

Charles VI (easy)

Q1 The Mad
Q2 42
Q3 Isabeau of Bavaria
Q4 Insanity
Q5 Louis I, Duke of Orléans
Q6 1407
Q7 Lancastrian War
Q8 Burgundy
Q9 Henry V
Q10 Masquerade ball

Charles VI (expert)

Q1 11
Q2 Armagnac faction and Burgundian faction
Q3 Henry V of England
Q4 Joanna of Bourbon
Q5 Hôtel Saint-Pol
Q6 Philip van Artevelde
Q7 Michel Pintoin
Q8 Richard II of England
Q9 1415
Q10 Glass delusion

Henry VI of England (easy)

Q1 Notre Dame
Q2 1
Q3 Catholic
Q4 Burned at the stake
Q5 The Wars of the Roses
Q6 Lancaster
Q7 3
Q8 Madness
Q9 English Channel
Q10 St Paul's Cathedral

Henry VI of England (average)

Q1 Margaret of Anjou
Q2 Tower of London
Q3 2
Q4 Westminster Abbey
Q5 Edward of Westminster, Prince of Wales
Q6 Second Battle of St Albans
Q7 Windsor Castle
Q8 Louis XI of France
Q9 9 months
Q10 Hundred Years' War

Henry VI of England (expert)

Q1 Eton College; King's College, Cambridge; and All Souls College, Oxford
Q2 The Maid of Orléans
Q3 John of Lancaster, Duke of Bedford
Q4 1435
Q5 Duke of Suffolk
Q6 1450
Q7 The restoration of Henry VI in 1470
Q8 Her parents
Q9 Battle of Northampton
Q10 Maternal grandfather

Charles VII

Q1 Armagnac faction
Q2 Hundred Years' War
Q3 Siege of Orléans
Q4 Burned at the stake
Q5 1429
Q6 Calais
Q7 Henry VI of England
Q8 Kingdom of England and Duchy of Burgundy
Q9 Joan of Arc
Q10 The Victorious (or the Well-Served)

Louis XI (easy)

Q1 The Prudent
Q2 1483
Q3 The Praguerie
Q4 Charlotte of Savoy
Q5 2
Q6 Edward IV
Q7 1
Q8 Old Swiss Confederacy
Q9 Orléans
Q10 Anne of France

Louis XI (expert)

Q1 1475
Q2 Charles the Bold, Duke of Burgundy
Q3 *The Hunchback of Notre-Dame*
Q4 Order of Saint Michael
Q5 League of the Public Weal
Q6 Spider
Q7 Merchant
Q8 Dauphin of France
Q9 House of Stewart (later Stuart)
Q10 Bourges Cathedral

Charles VIII

Q1 The Affable
Q2 13
Q3 Hit his head on a door lintel
Q4 Edward V of England
Q5 The Mad War
Q6 His sister, Anne of France
Q7 Brittany
Q8 1494
Q9 Cousin
Q10 Château d'Amboise

Louis XII (easy)

Q1 Naples
Q2 Charles, Duke of Orléans
Q3 Mary Tudor
Q4 Battle of Saint-Aubin-du-Cormier
Q5 First Italian War
Q6 Alexander VI
Q7 Milan
Q8 Father of the People
Q9 1508
Q10 Knight

Louis XII (expert)

Q1 Joan of France
Q2 1499–1504
Q3 Basilica of Saint-Denis
Q4 Father-in-law and cousin
Q5 1498
Q6 *The Prince*
Q7 1500
Q8 Republic of Venice
Q9 Claude of France
Q10 Maximilian Sforza

Francis I (easy)

Q1 Charles, Count of Angoulême
Q2 2
Q3 Château de Chambord
Q4 *Mona Lisa*
Q5 Explorer
Q6 Pale of Calais
Q7 Suleiman I
Q8 Cognac
Q9 Francis III, Duke of Brittany
Q10 The arts

Francis I (expert)

Q1 Henry VIII of England
Q2 Claude of France
Q3 1537
Q4 Hôtel de Ville
Q5 1515-1547
Q6 Charles V, Holy Roman Emperor
Q7 New York City
Q8 1543
Q9 The Catholic Church
Q10 Mérindol

Henry II

Q1 Jousting
Q2 Spain
Q3 Italian War of 1551–1559
Q4 Pale of Calais
Q5 1547–1559
Q6 Surgeon
Q7 Protestants
Q8 Mary, Queen of Scots
Q9 10
Q10 3

Francis II

Q1 Mary, Queen of Scots
Q2 16
Q3 1559-60
Q4 Artist
Q5 Scotland
Q6 Catherine de' Medici
Q7 1560
Q8 Charles, Cardinal of Lorraine
Q9 Huguenots
Q10 Toby Regbo

Charles IX

Q1 Brother
Q2 Huguenots
Q3 1572
Q4 La Rochelle
Q5 1560–1574
Q6 Tuberculosis
Q7 French Wars of Religion
Q8 1573
Q9 Catholics and Huguenots
Q10 Charles de Valois, Duke of Angoulême

Henry III

Q1 Henry II of France
Q2 Polish–Lithuanian Commonwealth
Q3 1573
Q4 Francis, Duke of Anjou
Q5 Henry III of France, Henry of Navarre and Henry of Guise
Q6 Jacques Clément
Q7 House of Valois
Q8 Château de Saint-Cloud
Q9 Guillaume Bérard
Q10 Favourites of Henry III

Henry IV (easy)

Q1 III
Q2 The Great
Q3 Bourbon
Q4 Assassinated
Q5 Antoine of Navarre
Q6 Protestant
Q7 Edict of Nantes
Q8 Acadia
Q9 Voltaire
Q10 Navarre

Henry IV (expert)

Q1 François Ravaillac
Q2 Louis IX of France (Saint Louis)
Q3 *Vive le roi Henri*
Q4 Margaret of Valois
Q5 1589–1610
Q6 Chartres Cathedral
Q7 Architecture
Q8 Philip II of Spain
Q9 Paris
Q10 French Wars of Religion

Louis XIII

Q1 II
Q2 His mother, Marie de' Medici
Q3 Italy
Q4 Cardinal Richelieu
Q5 *The Three Musketeers*
Q6 Charles d'Albert
Q7 Anne of Austria
Q8 Witchcraft
Q9 Thirty Years' War
Q10 The Netherlands

Louis XIV (easy)

Q1 The Sun King
Q2 72
Q3 Cardinal Mazarin
Q4 Palace of Versailles
Q5 Civil wars
Q6 Huguenots
Q7 Iron mask
Q8 Franco-Dutch War
Q9 Nine Years' War
Q10 2

Louis XIV (average)

Q1 Charles II of Spain
Q2 The Netherlands
Q3 Great-grandson
Q4 Anne of Austria
Q5 Paris
Q6 Architecture
Q7 Maria Theresa of Spain
Q8 Philip V of Spain
Q9 Germany
Q10 11

Louis XIV (expert)

Q1 England, Sweden and the Dutch Republic
Q2 War of the Reunions
Q3 1711
Q4 Château de Saint-Germain-en-Laye
Q5 Order of Saint Louis
Q6 Treaty of Aix-la-Chapelle
Q7 1708
Q8 Louisiana
Q9 Nine Years' War
Q10 Mistress

Louis XV (easy)

Q1 Bourbon
Q2 The Beloved
Q3 Great grandson
Q4 5
Q5 Chief Minister
Q6 War of the Austrian Succession
Q7 Spain and the United Kingdom
Q8 United Kingdom
Q9 0
Q10 Marie Leszczyńska

Louis XV (average)

Q1 Philippe II, Duke of Orléans
Q2 Louis XIV of France
Q3 Corsica
Q4 Napoléon Bonaparte
Q5 Louis, Dauphin of France
Q6 Poland
Q7 Palace of Versailles
Q8 Burgundy
Q9 Prussia
Q10 Physician

Louis XV (expert)

Q1 1756-63
Q2 Marie Adélaïde of Savoy
Q3 Louise Élisabeth of France
Q4 Decoration
Q5 Naval
Q6 Austria
Q7 1756
Q8 Robert-François Damiens
Q9 Pennsylvania
Q10 1715-74

Louis XVI (easy)

Q1 Citizen Louis Capet
Q2 1793
Q3 French Revolution
Q4 Guillotined
Q5 Austria
Q6 Land
Q7 Economist
Q8 USA
Q9 *Ancien Régime*
Q10 3

Louis XVI (average)

Q1 Marie Antoinette
Q2 Charles-Henri Sanson
Q3 1783
Q4 Bastille
Q5 The National Assembly
Q6 1791
Q7 French First Republic
Q8 Tuileries Palace
Q9 Louis Joseph, Dauphin of France
Q10 Maria Josepha of Saxony

Louis XVI (expert)

Q1 1775
Q2 Bernard-René Jourdan de Launay
Q3 French Constitution of 1791
Q4 Marie Thérèse of France
Q5 Edict of Tolerance
Q6 The Declaration of the Rights of Man and of the Citizen
Q7 1774
Q8 Axel von Fersen the Younger
Q9 Ernestine Lambriquet
Q10 Place de la Concorde

Louis XVII

Q1 10
Q2 Duke of Normandy
Q3 Palace of Versailles
Q4 Louis-Charles
Q5 Heart
Q6 Shoemaker
Q7 Louis Joseph, Dauphin of France
Q8 Son
Q9 Portrait painter
Q10 The Paris Temple

Napoléon Bonaparte (easy)

Q1 Corsica
Q2 Emperor of the French
Q3 2
Q4 111 days
Q5 First French Empire
Q6 Egypt
Q7 1799
Q8 7
Q9 Holy Roman Empire
Q10 Austrian Empire

Napoléon Bonaparte (average)

Q1 Notre-Dame
Q2 Empress Joséphine
Q3 13 Vendémiaire
Q4 First Consul
Q5 Arthur Wellesley, Duke of Wellington
Q6 1805
Q7 *Grande Armée*
Q8 The Battle of Friedland
Q9 His brother, Joseph Bonaparte
Q10 Iberian Peninsula

Napoléon Bonaparte (expert)

Q1 1803-15
Q2 Francis II
Q3 Battle of Jena–Auerstedt
Q4 A blockade
Q5 1812
Q6 Elba and Saint Helena
Q7 Bourbon
Q8 Napoleonic Code
Q9 Hôtel national des Invalides
Q10 Letizia Ramolino

Louis XVIII (easy)

Q1 The Desired
Q2 Brother
Q3 Count of Provence
Q4 Marie Joséphine of Savoy
Q5 0
Q6 Vienna
Q7 1815
Q8 Bourbon Restoration
Q9 An army
Q10 Belgium

Louis XVIII (expert)

Q1 68
Q2 1815
Q3 *Chambre introuvable*
Q4 A constitution
Q5 Charles Maurice de Talleyrand-Périgord
Q6 Gosfield Hall
Q7 Property
Q8 The Hundred Days
Q9 Brother
Q10 Basilica of Saint-Denis

Napoleon II

Q1 1815
Q2 Reichstadt
Q3 Marie Louise, Duchess of Parma
Q4 Schönbrunn Palace
Q5 21
Q6 Tuberculosis
Q7 Austrian army
Q8 Step-father
Q9 Cousin
Q10 1811

Charles X (easy)

Q1 Artois
Q2 Brother
Q3 An ultra-royalist
Q4 Charles Ferdinand, Duke of Berry
Q5 Rheims
Q6 A parliamentary body
Q7 Algeria
Q8 Prime Minister
Q9 July Revolution
Q10 Italy

Charles X (expert)

Q1 Paris Opera
Q2 Jules de Polignac
Q3 1824-30
Q4 Kostanjevica Monastery
Q5 Maria Theresa of Savoy
Q6 1830
Q7 *Le National*
Q8 Henri, Count of Chambord
Q9 1825
Q10 1836

Louis Antoine

Q1 20 minutes
Q2 Dauphin of France
Q3 Louis XIX
Q4 Angoulême
Q5 Palace of Versailles
Q6 Marie Thérèse of France
Q7 Son
Q8 1844
Q9 His nephew, Henri, Count of Chambord
Q10 Edinburgh

Henri, Count of Chambord

Q1 V
Q2 Charles Ferdinand, Duke of Berry
Q3 Tuileries Palace
Q4 Grandson
Q5 Bourbon
Q6 1830
Q7 Legitimists
Q8 0
Q9 Marie-Caroline of Bourbon-Two Sicilies, Duchess of Berry
Q10 Austro-Hungarian Empire

Louis Philippe I (easy)

Q1 Louis Philippe II, Duke of Orléans
Q2 1793
Q3 Orléans
Q4 King of the French
Q5 Maria Amalia of Naples and Sicily
Q6 1848 Revolution
Q7 July Monarchy
Q8 Orléanists
Q9 England
Q10 Palais-Royal

Louis Philippe I (expert)

Q1 François Guizot
Q2 Ferdinand Philippe, Duke of Orléans
Q3 1830-48
Q4 July Revolution
Q5 Chapelle royale de Dreux
Q6 Giuseppe Marco Fieschi
Q7 76
Q8 Princess Elizabeth of the United Kingdom
Q9 10
Q10 French Second Republic

Napoleon III (easy)

Q1 Nephew
Q2 President of France
Q3 1848 Revolution
Q4 Second French Empire
Q5 Franco-Prussian War
Q6 Russia
Q7 Suez Canal
Q8 United Kingdom
Q9 Mexico
Q10 1870

Napoleon III (average)

Q1 1848-52
Q2 Georges-Eugène Haussmann
Q3 Maximilian I of Mexico
Q4 Otto von Bismarck
Q5 Battle of Sedan
Q6 French Third Republic
Q7 Eugénie de Montijo
Q8 England
Q9 Louis Bonaparte
Q10 1851

Napoleon III (expert)

Q1 Treaty of Frankfurt
Q2 St Michael's Abbey, Farnborough
Q3 Napoléon, Prince Imperial
Q4 Louis-Eugène Cavaignac
Q5 Treaty of Paris (1856)
Q6 Ems Dispatch
Q7 Government of National Defence
Q8 Eugène Viollet-le-Duc
Q9 Germany and Italy
Q10 Second Italian War of Independence

Also by B.R. Egginton

Non-fiction

Edward VI: England's Boy King

Edward VI's Chronicle (Edward VI)

Richard II: The Tyranny of the White Hart

The Princes in the Tower: An Enigma… 500 Years in the Making

Nicholas II: The Fall of the Romanovs

Henry Hotze: The Master of Confederate Diplomacy

Historiography for Beginners

Archaeology for Beginners

Twelve Olympians: The Greek Pantheon Made Easy

History Essay Writing Basics: For High School and Undergraduate Students

Shorthand SOS: Learn Teeline Shorthand FAST

Public Affairs for Journalists: Concise Edition

Ice Hockey Rulebook

Fiction

The Sixth Number

A Kingdom of Our Own

The Chronicles of Ascension

History Quest: The Plot

The Prince and the Pauper: Annotated Edition (Mark Twain)

Trivia

The Ultimate History Quiz

The Ultimate Mythology Quiz

The Ultimate US Presidents Quiz

The Ultimate British Prime Ministers Quiz

The Ultimate British Royal Navy Quiz

The Ultimate English Monarchs Quiz